One
BOOK
One
STORY

One BOOK *One* STORY

THE BIBLE'S BIG PICTURE

DAVID W. EDWARDS

XULON PRESS

Xulon Press
2301 Lucien Way #415
Maitland, FL 32751
407.339.4217
www.xulonpress.com

Printed in the United States of America.

ISBN-13: 9781545604809

TO MY PARENTS, IRA & MARGARET,
who taught me to love the Bible
and to live by it.

TO MY GIRLFRIEND
to whom I have had the joy
of being married for 40 years.

ACKNOWLEDGEMENTS

MOST OF THE MATERIAL in this book was written first as sermons. It would be unfair to ignore the contribution and encouragement of Safe Harbor Church of the Nazarene– a wonderful group of people who listen and learn, and then encourage their pastor. I am fortunate to have been able to preach the Word of God to people who tell me to preach until I'm done. If God has given me a word, they want to hear it. Would that every pastor was surrounded by such people.

I need to thank those who took the time and effort to read and critique early versions of this work. They gave valuable assistance which made this better than I could have done alone. My colleagues in ministry, Ray Finch and Michael Hull, took time out of more important tasks to help. My parents read the manuscript and encouraged me to continue. They helped work out a few kinks. I especially appreciate the work of editing and critiquing and the many valuable suggestions offered by my daughter Kristina and her husband Alex Ferguson. I've learned that while a book may be the work of a single author, it is never the work of a single person.

TABLE OF CONTENTS

INTRODUCTION

I AM PROPOSING IN THIS book that the Bible is a single book rather than a library, and that it tells a single story. But we are not accustomed to reading the Bible that way. We "slice and dice" the scriptures, and parse the sentences, and end up preaching a fragmented story. We end up, in some cases, what I have described as "blender theology." We misunderstand the *parts* of that story because we have lost sight of the *whole*. But I've discovered that each of the smaller stories tell that same larger story to a smaller audience in a more intimate setting. It has been my goal over the years to connect the parts of the story and try to tell them from within their larger Biblical and historical context – to set Jesus' birth, for example, not only in the context of the Genesis promise and Isaiah's prophecy, but also in the context of Alexander the Great and the fragmented empire he left. To that end, I believe, it's time for a new look at the old Book.

1

THE TRIVIALIZATION
OF SCRIPTURE

I N 2004, A GAME show contestant named Ken Jennings became famous. He was a contestant on *Jeopardy* for 75 consecutive appearances and won a total of $3,196,300 (trivia: the most until 2005, when Brad Rutter surpassed him with winnings of $4,555,102). But the number of appearances and the amount won were the result of Jennings' unusual ability–the ability to recall volumes of trivial information.

The game show *Jeopardy* is unique in that it provides answers and contestants must provide the questions. To provide a question, contestants are required to push a button–the quickest being the one to respond. Successful contestants must be quick and knowledgeable and their knowledge must cover a wide variety of topics from mathematics and spelling to world history, current events, and pop culture. Most of what they must know, however, comes in the form of what is commonly known today as "factoids", or trivia – bits of information that have little use but may be of interest. The main use of trivia, however, is for people who wish to demonstrate their knowledge of useless information, and to appear intelligent.

Games shows, such as *Jeopardy*, reflect an industry that began with the advent of commercial radio and grew with the invention of television as an entertainment medium. Programs such as Groucho Marx's *You Bet Your Life* (from 1947-1960), *The $64,000 Question* (aired 1955-1958), *The Price is Right* (aired from 1956 to 2007), offered prizes to contestants who could guess the answers to obscure questions or the manufacturer's suggested retail prices on products that were never sold for those amounts. The "substance" of these game shows is trivia.

Table games have been invented to take advantage of the fascination with useless information. Parlor games such as *Trivial Pursuit®*, with several different subject formats, have proven to be quite popular in recent years. An online search for "trivia games" yields hundreds of games, locations, and articles. Many organizations use trivia games in what I believe to be a misguided effort to teach science, history, literature, safety, environmentalism, or even religion.

I grew up on what might be described as Bible trivia. We played travel games involving Bible characters, places, and events. Sunday School classes not only taught us the Books of the Bible and selected memory verses, but we learned how many verses, chapters, and even words were in the Bible, which was the longest, the shortest, the middle verse, chapter or book. In short, trivia games test your knowledge of unimportant information, factoids, irrelevancies, and meaning-less minutiae.

Bible trivia may be useful if it sparks curiosity or serves as an introduction to more in-depth teaching. But trivia is shallow information at best. We may learn a lot about a particular topic, but we will never learn anything useful. That is, we may learn a lot about the Bible but trivia does not teach us the content of the Bible. We may learn a lot about Christianity but trivia does not teach us how to be Christian. There may be biblical Ken Jennings's but they will not be the people we turn to when we need real help.

This is to point out a fallacy and a failure of the Church and of many Christians: that we tend to treat the Bible as a storehouse of religious infor-mation, a collection of morality plays or children's stories, or a theological dictionary. Though many would deny that they do this, most Bible studies are more or less just a search for information or Bible trivia. The Bible is dissected and the details of particular verses, parables, or events, are "studied" so that they might serve as examples or to teach Christians how they ought to act or react in any given situation. Some Bibles are printed with a list of verses to read in particular situations – when grieving, when sick, when depressed, etc.

Most Bible studies, indeed most sermons, take the Bible in small bites. We memorize by the verse or paragraph. For example, many people have memorized "The Lord's Prayer" and many churches include it in their liturgy. But the prayer itself is lifted out of its context. People are some-times surprised to learn that Jesus continued his teaching and commented on the content of that prayer.

The prayer "Jesus taught us to pray" includes the petition, "Forgive us our debts (trespasses) as we forgive our debtors (those who trespass against us)." We often do not realize that the two versions of this prayer, over which we sometimes argue, are from two different gospels – one from Matthew, the other from Luke. One has an economic bent in that it refers to debts owed rather than sins committed.

But in Matthew's version the issue of forgiveness is continued. Jesus concludes the prayer and then says, *"For if you forgive people their wrongdoing, your heavenly Father will forgive you as well. But if you don't forgive people, your Father will not forgive your wrongdoing"* (Matthew 6:14-15, HCSB). In other words, Jesus specifically lifts out the issue of forgiveness for additional teaching. Why? That question is seldom asked or answered in our memorization.

And we almost never delve into the meaning of *"thy kingdom come; thy will be done on earth as it is in heaven."* This single phrase is the key to the whole prayer. In truth, this should be known as "The Kingdom Prayer" rather than The Lord's Prayer.

Perhaps a more egregious misuse of Scripture is the almost ubiquitous quoting of John 8:32. I have seen it on television in the scripts of programs that have nothing whatever to do with Christianity. Television's fictional detectives declare to suspects that "the truth will set you free."

No, actually, the truth will not set you free. This may come as a surprise, but it really depends

ERRATA

on what the truth is. Telling the truth could land a criminal in prison. Telling the truth might end a philanderer's marriage and get him tied up with years of alimony payments. Telling the truth will get a tax cheater years in prison and thousands of dollars in debt.

But the more important point is this: that is not what Jesus actually said! He did not make a blanket statement that "the truth will set you free." Those six words are not even the complete sentence. They are, in fact, a small part of what Jesus said – even if we take only the one full sentence (actually two sentences).

"If you continue in my word, you really are my disciples. You will know the truth, and the truth will set you free" (John 6:31-32, HCSB). In many translations, the word "then" is inserted at the beginning of the second sentence because it is implied by the structure of the two sentences in the Greek. There are two conditions to this "if/then" promise. *If* the first part is true, *then* the second part will be true; and *if* that part is true, *then* the last is true. The statement is really this: *If* you continue in my word, *then* you are my disciples, and *if* you are my disciples, *then* you will know the truth and *that* truth will set you free. Knowing the truth that frees is contingent upon obeying Jesus and being his disciple. It is simply not a true statement in its commonly-used and incomplete form.

That's the way a lot of people use the Bible. They take bits and pieces out of context, and twist them – often, I believe, not even knowing that this is what they are doing. It's one thing to do it in ignorance. It's quite another for a Christian, particularly a minister who should know better, to do it.

One of the most humorous examples is one that was relayed to me many years ago. I had engaged an evangelist for a revival campaign. He was somewhat elderly and had many years of experience in the church. He told me this story –

In the 1930s, there was a new women's hairstyle in fashion called a "topknot". It consisted of drawing long hair onto the top of one's head and forming it into a "bun". (In the 1960s, I had a school teacher who wore her hair in this fashion.) An elderly preacher took exception to the fashion and preached a sermon against it. He took his text from Matthew's gospel – Matthew 24:17 – these words (as the preacher quoted): "topknot come down".

The diligent student will find the verse, in the midst of Jesus preaching about "the end of the age", and read, *"Let him who is on the housetop not come down."* The old preacher did not quote the full verse, misspelled what he did use, and used it completely apart from it's context. It has nothing to do with hair or fashion. In fact, the preacher took half a word! This was not simple ignorant misuse, but a deliberate abuse of the Scripture.

Sadly, this kind of proof-texting is not uncommon. It is widely used as an evangelistic technique. When we deal falsely with the Scriptures, particularly in our attempts to win others to our faith, we betray less than honorable motives and a less than honest faith. My youngest daughter has always insisted that I include verse 17 when I quoted John 3:16 because it is an inseparable part of the thought (and context). Romans 3:23 and 6:23 are frequently used without regard to their context, and one of my pet peeves is the pervasive misuse of Jeremiah 29:11, regarding God's positive plans, apart from the context of warning and judgment regarding the sin that short-circuits God's good plan. Jeremiah was actually telling Israel, this is what God wants, what God intends, but because of your sin this is what you will get instead.

In fact, the usual evangelistic use of Scripture has often served to individualize the gospel. For example, we quote the maxim that "God has a wonderful plan for your life." But it is aimed at an individual, as if God's plan is all about individuals. Jeremiah 29:11 is one example, where the prophet relays the message from God: *"For I know the plans I have for you..."* But the point of the verse is that God's wonderful plan is meant for more than individual people, churches, or denominations.

One fallacy is that we treat the "you" of Scripture in the singular, when in point of fact the "you" of the Bible is almost always plural, what is referred to as a "corporate you". We would understand it better with a Southern accent, "y'all", as in "Do *y'all* not know that *all y'all* are God's sanctuary?" (1 Corinthians 3:16). Jeremiah 29:11 refers to God's wonderful plans for the *nation* of Judah ("For I know the plans I have for *y'all*"), and not to any specific individual in the nation (or the church, today).

It is not wrong to quote a single verse, so long as it is used appropriately in regard to its context. And we learn a lot from the "stories" and the lives of the people of Scripture. Bible study, whether verse by verse, chapter by chapter, or book by book, is valuable. But it leaves us short of understanding the Bible.

I grew up learning the Bible stories: stories of great men and women of faith: Joseph, Moses, Joshua, Gideon, Deborah, David, and the rest. They were great and greatly to be admired and imitated. They were set up as examples for me. And yet...

Children are not taught the whole story. They are taught, as I was, the best bits, the heroism, the faith, the miracles. But they are often not taught that these very same heroes were weak, immoral, and sometimes did stupid things. They are not taught that these great heroes of faith were also very (sometimes embarrassingly) human. Thus our picture of faith is skewed. When we fail, make mistakes, and display our own lack of faith, we have no one to serve as an example of redemption. We are not taught that God did not use these people because of their faith but often in spite of their lack of faith. God did not use these people because they were innately heroic but because they were afraid.

Let me give you just one example: Gideon.

At the beginning of the story Gideon is hiding, threshing wheat inside a winepress. Picture him hunkered down in a large bin, rubbing kernels of wheat between his hands to separate the grain from the chaff. He is not out in the open because he is afraid and hungry. Israel was, at the time, under the oppressive control of their neighbor, Midian. The Midianites had the unsettling habit of waiting for Israel to harvest and process their crops, and then swooping in and stealing the food. Gideon was trying to keep some of the crop hidden and safe for his family.

An angel appears and greets the timid farm boy, "Hail, mighty warrior!"

The irony is not lost on Gideon, who looks around for the "mighty warrior", and then responds with a "Who? Me?" Gideon is the youngest member of the weakest family in the smallest tribe of Israel. It might help us to imagine him as a skinny, awkward teenager – in modern terms, a geeky kid.

The angel tells Gideon that *he* is going to be the one to deliver Israel from her enemy, the enemy Gideon is hiding from. The boy responds by doing the only thing he knows to do – he brings lunch for the visitor. When he sets the lunch on a rock, fire springs up and burns the meal to ash. Okay, so maybe there *is* something to this.

God tells Gideon to tear down the altar to the Canaanite gods his family worships. In the middle of the night the boy sneaks out of his tent with a few of his friends (the Bible calls them "servants"). They climb the hill, tear down the altar, build another altar to God, and sacrifice two of the family's bulls – an expensive "loss" for which he does not have his father's permission. As a result, when the men of the village find out, Gideon's life is in jeopardy. The men want to kill him for his vandalism. Surprisingly, his father intervenes in his favor and Gideon lives to tremble another day.

But the boy is still not sure that he's doing the right thing, so he proposes a test. "If you are God, and if you really, really want me to do this, here's a sheep skin. I'll lay it on the ground and when the dew falls during the night, make the skin wet and the ground dry."

God does it and Gideon wrings out a pitcher full of water. Does Gideon have faith? Is he ready to trust God yet? No. He rationalizes that the skin might have attracted moisture, so he proposes another test, the reverse of the first: let the ground be wet and the fleece dry. God does it, and Gideon decides he has no choice but to obey.

We hear and read about so many Christians who refer to "putting out a fleece" as an act of faith. But it is really the reverse: Gideon put out the fleece because he did not believe. He put out the fleece hoping he had it all wrong and that he had an "out" from what he heard the angel saying. Gideon's fleece was an act of unbelief, delay and disobedience. It's like the Christian who says that "God told me..., but I need to pray about it." Why? They doubt. They don't believe. And if it were God who gave them the instruction, to whom are they going to pray? They are hoping God will change His mind.

As I read Judges 6 I do not see the hero I learned about in Sunday School. Instead I see a fearful, reluctant farm boy, carried along in a direction he does not want to go and making every effort to avoid it.

Can God use such a person? Of course, he can. Can God use us when we are afraid, faith-less, "geeky"? If we allow the story to tell itself the answer is a resounding yes! In fact, that is perhaps the most important lesson to learn from the story of Gideon. God does not require us to be people of great faith, nor to be people of great righteous-ness, nor to be highly talented. He only requires that we be willing to be made willing to be useful. He doesn't even require us to be successful, just to follow directions and keep going until he tells us to stop.

And so Gideon gathers an army– 32,000 men show up in answer to his summons. There is a great and powerful enemy and it will take a great and powerful army to defeat them. But God will have none of it and tells Gideon to release all who are afraid. 22,000 pack up and go home. Still too many, so God gives Gideon a test and 9,600 of them fail, leaving this "mighty warrior" with just 300 men.

Are these the best of the best? Are these the mightiest of the warriors? Probably not. The way this story is going these are probably also geeky teens, skinny kids who can barely lift a sword, which, by the way, they won't have anyway.

Because the entire battle plays out with Gideon's "soldiers" essentially unarmed. (No, I wasn't told that important detail, either!) The "army" of 300 is arrayed on the hills around the enemy camp. Each of the "soldiers" are to hide a torch inside a clay pot. They are also to have a "trumpet"–a *shofar* (ram's horn). At Gideon's signal, they are to break the pot and lift the torch with one hand. With the other hand they are to put the shofar to their mouth and blow. Only two talents are required here: to be able to hold a torch and to blow a trumpet – at the same time. Which hand is left to hold a sword? At Gideon's signal, his "army" broke their clay pots and lifted out the torch and started to sound their trumpets. The startled enemy army, imagining their doom, began to flail their own swords in the darkness of the night, killing each other and fleeing desperately from their imagined enemy. Then, at the sight of the panicked army, the "geek army" ran down the hill, picked up abandoned swords and began to chase their frightened enemy.

It's actually more like a scene from a Mel Brooks movie. These are not heroes, mighty men with swords. These are geeky boys with trumpets. They don't win anything, except perhaps an award for audacity. It's more like catching lizards in the rocks than fighting a battle against seasoned warriors.

Can children learn from the "stories" of the Bible? Of course, they can. But we must be faithful to the story and not make it out to be more (or less) than it is. We must be careful to depict the "heroes" in our story-telling as they actually were and not as idealized "men of faith." The story of Gideon teaches us that God can even use geeky teenage boys who are afraid of their own shadows. God can use reluctant servants.

The Big Picture

But while all of that may have some value in limited situations, it occurs to me that it is not the best way to know the Bible or the best way to understand the Bible. In fact, while many Christians may know the minutiae of Scripture, may know when, where, and by whom all the books and letters were written, and the essential "message" of each, most do not know that the Bible itself contains a single meta-narrative. There is a "big picture", an account of God's ultimate plan.

My wife likes jigsaw puzzles. The more pieces and the more challenging the better. But she does not linger long over any single piece. The point is to put it where is belongs, to fit 1,000 variously-shaped pieces into a single large scene. Each piece is important, of course, and if one is missing the picture is incomplete. But the joy of assembling a jigsaw puzzle is in discovering "the big picture" in all it's wonder.

You see, the Bible is not just a collection of books nor a collection of miscellaneous moral tales. Yes, I know that there are 66 books written by forty authors over a period of some 1500 years. That is the method and the structure, but it is not what the Bible is. The Bible is one book with one story, the story of God's creation from beginning to end. There is a plan and the 66 parts fit together like pieces of a grand puzzle. There is value in studying the pieces, but, as with the jigsaw puzzle, we need to study the pieces to see where they fit. Then we need to put them together so that we can see the whole picture.

2

IN THE BEGINNING

Genesis 6:1-8

I REMEMBER ONE OF MY first sermons. I was a teenager with a fresh call of God on my life, and I was excited to begin. Like a child learning to walk, this is a slow beginning with a lot of stumbles and failures along the way. And it was not as easy as it looked. I preached everything I knew, the whole Bible, from Genesis to Revelation, in about ten minutes – and ran out of things to say. I probably don't need to tell you that, as it turned out, I didn't really know very much.

Well, we're going to take a rather quick journey – not *that* quick – through the Bible in these pages, Genesis to Revelation. Not everything I know now, by the way, because I've learned a few more things, but we'll try to hit the most important things.

The trajectory of the first part of this book is the "meta-narrative" of the Bible – the Big Picture. Rather than look at a single book or trace a single theme we're going to look at where we came from, where we've stumbled along the way, where we're going, and how God has worked to keep his plan on track in spite of human failure.

Our steps on this journey are the Flood, the Exodus, the Exile, the Word, the Water, the Spirit, and the Resolution. Let's start at the Beginning.

The Bible begins with a Grand Plan. God, complete in Himself, creates. One of the attributes of God is that he is Creative.

A few years ago, a group from my church went to the Hawaiian island of Maui to help build a church. While we were there, members of that church treated us to some of the local attractions. One of those was a ride on the Atlantis submarine in Lahaina. The Atlantis took us to the bottom of the ocean about a half mile from shore. When the captain stopped the sub, he turned on powerful outside lights. We were amazed to see so many varieties of brightly-colored fish – reds, blues, and yellows in amazing patterns. Sunlight does not penetrate to the depth of 150 feet where we were, which means that even if they could see color, fish would not be able to see it at that depth.

Sunlight does not penetrate, mankind does not live at that depth, fish cannot see it, so why would color even "evolve" there?

On vacation one year, my wife and I saw a carpet of white flowers covering a golf course fairway. We went to get a closer look, knelt down and looked through a magnifying glass, to discover an astonishing variety of patterns traced in purple on these snowy flowers. Why? It is so fine that we would not see it without a deliberate look.

The universe has been described as vast and empty and someone once called it "wasted space". But if you gaze upward at the stars, you hear the psalmist whisper in your ear, *"The heavens declare the glory of God"* (Psalm 19:1). Astronomers focused the Hubble Space Telescope on a small portion of distance space that appeared to be empty, and made a long exposure photograph of that pinpoint. What they discovered was amazing – thousands more galaxies, nebulae, and objects never before known and otherwise invisible from earth. "Empty space" is not empty.

Not only is God creative, but his creation is extravagant – in human terms wasteful, lavish, abundant. If you're paying attention to the world around, you will see grandeur and majesty and you will see tiny and intricate beauty. Nature is wildly profuse with life and beauty. He did not merely create a rose, he created a rose with the ability to manifest in hundreds of shapes, colors, and patterns. His creation is incredibly varied- simply overwhelming in variety and intricacy – thousands upon thousands of species of flowers and plants, insects and fish, sea and land animals, and birds.

God created it all with such intricacy and minute care that we marvel at the patterns we find under the most powerful microscopes. Things that are too tiny for us to see and enjoy are nonetheless amazingly intricate and beautiful. Whenever

I take the time to contemplate such things, all I can do is ask why. Why would God create billions upon billions of stars? Why would God create creatures with color where there is no light? Why would God create such an astounding variety of creatures? Would not one kind of ant, one kind of bee, one kind of cat or dog, one kind of bird be sufficient? So when we discover hundreds of species of ants, thousands of species of birds, and animals and plants equipped precisely for their environment, we stand in amazement.

They all share the incomprehensibly vast library of information-coded DNA, but each with it's own unique arrangement. We study genetics to learn how things are made and the science of epigenetics to learn about traits inherited apart from genetics and that can't be explained by changes in the DNA sequence. We study chemistry to learn about the materials from which things are made and how they combine. It's not enough to simply have instructions on how to build the house; you must also have the materials to build the house. DNA can tell us how to build and what materials to use, but DNA doesn't account for the materials of life. And so God called a world into being, filled with his glory, abundant, lavish, and extravagant. (Genesis 1).

Then he hand-formed humans, stamped them with his divine fingerprint and breathed his own breath into them. I love the way Genesis 2:7 reads – *"And God formed the man from the dust of the ground, and breathed into his nostrils the spirit of life, and the man became a living soul."* The man himself was created with a genetic code that made possible a virtually infinite variety of skin, hair, and eye color, finger prints more varied than snowflakes, and each eye and ear unique. Today, more than seven billion humans live on this earth–no two of them exactly alike. Endowed with life, created to live, they are blessed with the ability to enjoy both the Creator and the opulent beauty of creation. God placed the man in a garden, described as *Eden*, a Hebrew word meaning "bliss" or "delight"–a delightful place, filled with the exquisite perfection of God's love.

God is to be worshiped, but he has angels for that. Isaiah described the throne with God surrounded by worshiping angels, crying out to one another, *"Holy, holy, holy, is the LORD God Almighty"* (Isaiah 6:1-4). Man was to be different, the Psalmist says, *a little lower than the heavenly beings* (Psalm 8:5), but *crowned with glory and honor*. Not mandated to worship, but given the choice to love and worship freely. Love is not love if it is coerced. This bit of creation could not be a puppet or a machine. It must be free, and its love freely offered.

And so God planted a tree – two trees, actually, in that garden. One, the Tree of Life, from which the man could eat freely. The other, the Tree of the Knowledge of Good and Evil, from with the man must not eat. To eat that fruit was to know evil and when Adam and his wife chose to eat that fruit, death entered the story. Sin in the form of selfish desire blossomed into rebellion, disobedience, and *in Adam all die* (1 Corinthians 15:22). *The wages of sin is death* (Romans 6:23). It is interesting to note that they do not appear to have thought to eat of the Tree of Life, and now God exiles them from the garden, from that magnificent paradise, lest they choose to eat that fruit. God pronounced a curse, with a hidden blessing (Genesis 3:15), clothed them with skins from a sacrificed animal (Genesis 3:21), and sent them away, with an angel guarding *the way to the tree of life* (Genesis 3). Remember those things – the blessing, the sacrifice, the tree – for they are all part of "the rest of the story".

Adam and Eve go out into the frightening, no-longer-paradise world where death reigns and they are about to get a powerful lesson. In time they have a son, Cain, who grows up to be a farmer working the soil. Then they have a second son, Abel, who grows up to be a shepherd. Because their parents knew God and have perhaps told the sad story of why we live here and not there, and what life used to be like, the two boys bring an offering to the Lord.

There's a lot here we don't understand – why Abel's offering of fatness was pleasing to God while Cain's offering of "some" produce was not. Apparently, even then there was a right way and a wrong way to worship God. Some worship, some offerings, are acceptable; others are not. So we ask, was Abel sincere and Cain not? Was one an offering of "firsts" and the other an offering of "seconds"? And how did they know that God was pleased with the one and displeased with the other? There was an old Sunday School teaching picture that depicted the smoke from Abel's offering rising straight up while the smoke from Cain's offering hovered near the ground. Preachers read an awful lot into this story. What we do know is that Cain became angry with his brother. God tried to warn

Cain of the danger of anger – how murderous thoughts grow from the seeds of irritation; how sin always begins in the heart and must be controlled there before it burst out. Jesus would warn that *"Anyone who is angry with his brother will be subject to judgment"* (Matthew 5:22). God warned Cain, *"Sin is crouching at your door; it desires to have you, but you must master it"* (Genesis 4:7).

He didn't. Instead he was mastered by it, hatched a plan, led his brother out into the field and brutally murdered him. *"Am I my brother's keeper?"* His pretended innocence did not fool God. Again, God pronounces a curse, the ground would no longer be fertile for Cain, and he would be a "restless wanderer". Another exile, and the seeds of sin, planted in the garden, have taken root (Genesis 4).

The imprint of God in mankind fades. *When God created man, he made him in the **likeness of God**.... When Adam had lived 130 years, he had a son in **his own likeness**, in his own image* (Genesis 5:1-3). We no longer reflect God's likeness, the *imago dei*; now we reflect our parents. Born in sin, conceived in iniquity (Psalm 51:5), our genetic make-up comes half from our father and half from our mother, so that we look like them.

Let me digress just a moment. Some people have read Psalm 51:5–*Behold, I was shapen in iniquity; and in sin did my mother conceive me* (KJV)- to mean that the act of procreation, sex, is a bad thing and dirty, to be avoided and condemned because it is the way "original sin" is passed on. It is part of a dualistic (or gnostic) view of the world that the physical is corrupt and evil, and the spirit is good.

Even sex within marriage has been viewed by some as a necessary evil. That's not at all what this means. The sexual relationship is the highest form of human physical intimacy and a precious gift a husband and wife bestow upon one another. It is the deepest physical expression of love between two people – which is why it should be saved for marriage and not spent as a cheap commodity. We do not hide it because it is dirty, but because it is precious. The "conceived in iniquity" bit is a reference to the mystery of sinful humanity – somehow, quite apart from the physical, we inherit a sinful nature. Somehow, apart from genetics, we know sin and we know that *all have sinned and fall short of the glory God intended* (Romans 3:23).

The seed of rebellion planted in the garden begins to flower. It is a descendant of Cain, just five generations, who boasts, *"I have killed a man for wounding me... If Cain is avenged seven times, then Lamech seventy-seven times"* (Genesis 4:23-24). That, by the way, is the last we hear of Cain's descendants. But the attitude continues. Sin does not infect Cain's line alone.

The story now turns to Adam and Eve's third son, Seth. It was in his day that *"men began to call on the name of the LORD*[1]*"* (Genesis 4:24). By no stretch

---

[1] In some translations the word Lord is rendered LORD in places where the unpronounceable name of God, known as the Tetragrammaton and transliterated into English as YHWH, appears. It is unpronounceable for two reasons: 1) in the Hebrew it has no vowel "points" to direct how it should be spoken, and 2) it is considered to be too holy for the human mouth to speak. The English *Jehovah* was created by interposing the vowel points from *Adonai* into

of the imagination does that mean they were good, anymore than "religious" people today are necessarily good. Religious does not equal righteous or even moral. Even so, mankind continued to invent new ways of evil. It came to a head here: *The LORD saw how great man's wickedness had become, and that every inclination of the thoughts of his heart was only evil all the time* (Genesis 6:5). Notice the superlatives the writer of Genesis used to express the drastic nature of what God saw in mankind – great wickedness, every inclination, only evil, all the time. How far we have fallen!

Maybe God had made a mistake in creating mankind in the first place. Maybe this was not such a good idea after all. Maybe he should just wipe it all out, clean the slate, and start over.

There is one who walks with God, he also of the fifth generation, Enoch (Genesis 6:22-23). God took Enoch out of the world, but not before his son Methuselah was born. Methuselah had a son, another Lamech. There was something good in him, it seems. Lamech had a son, whom he named, "Comforter". Lamech's explanation: *"Perhaps he will comfort us in the labor and painful toil... caused by the ground the LORD has cursed"* (Genesis 5:29). "Comforter". Remember that. It is an important part of the story. But we know him as Noah. And

---

the Tetragrammaton and substituting J for Y (Hebrew has no J). Recent scholarship suggests that the nearest pronunciation of YHWH would be "Yahweh". See "God, Names of" II:C The Covenant Name in The International Standard Bible Encyclopedia, Volume 2 (Grand Rapids: William B. Eerdmans, 1982)

as God was contemplating the idea of wiping it all out and starting over with a clean slate, he noticed Noah – *Noah found favor in the eyes of the LORD* (Genesis 6:8). *Noah was a righteous man, blameless among the people of his time, and he walked with God* (Genesis 6:9). Blameless, not faultless, as we'll see, but still a righteous man who walked with God. The *starting over* idea was still in God's mind, but there was something in his good creation that could be salvaged. There was a remnant, some good that remained, like a diamond in a coal mine.

And the coal mine was very dark: *Now the earth was corrupt in God's sight and was full of violence. God saw how corrupt the earth had become, for all the people on earth had corrupted their ways* (Genesis 6:11). Except Noah. So God told Noah his plan – he was going to begin again. Noah would be the new Adam. First though, God had to wipe out the evil and corruption, the rot of human immorality. There would come a flood, like nothing ever seen, and Noah was given instructions on how to build a great floating zoo. Animals would come, with an instinct for survival, two by two in most cases, seven by seven in others (Genesis 7:3). And Noah was to take his family – his wife, three sons and their wives – into the boat for safety.

The rains came, the underground springs welled up, and the flood covered the entire world, destroying everything. Except Noah. The mountains were covered to a depth of twenty feet – there was not a safe, or dry, place. Except in the safety of the ark. The rains fell for forty days, and everything, every living creature, men and animals, even the birds were *wiped from the earth* (Genesis

7:23). What God had declared good, even very good (Genesis 1:31), had become so perverse that the only way God in his wisdom could see was to begin again.

In time, the waters receded and plants once again began to grow. God remembered Noah, set the boat in a safe place, and opened the door. There is one more interesting note we must make: After the ark came to rest on the mountains of Ararat and the mountains themselves became visible, Noah waited forty days. He sent out a raven and then a dove. After the dove returned Noah waited another seven days and again sent out the dove, for a total of about seven weeks. When the dove did not return, Noah knew it had found a roost and that it was safe to leave the shelter of the ark. There was another "first day" (Genesis 8:13) as mankind again began to settle the earth.

Noah's first act upon leaving the ark was to build an altar and make a sacrifice of worship to God. It was a pleasing sacrifice to God, and God responded to the goodness in Noah's heart with a promise, a new blessing of fruitfulness, a signed covenant–the rainbow is God's signature, God's promise to never again destroy the earth in this way. He is a God of New Beginnings; a God of Second Chances. Remember that, for it forms the very heart of the story we are telling.

Remember, also, the forty days of rain and the seven weeks of waiting. Remember the first day, for it, too, is significant. Remember the ark, and the dove. Remember the remnant of the faithful. We will see them again.

There are those who want to mythologize the story of Noah; who suggest that it was borrowed from the mythology of some other culture. The story of Noah is similar is some ways to the Epic of Gilgamesh and to other flood myths. There is one significant difference: Noah is not presented as a hero or a savior. And the plan is one of redemption, not simply survival. Noah does not "save" the human race for he himself was one of those saved. And in the aftermath of the flood, Noah is still quite human–he is not elevated to the status of a god.

There are also those who want to take the story as literal history. Ark replicas, both miniature and full sized, have been constructed to teach about the "historicity" of the flood and the historical accuracy of the Bible. Whether true or not, this is also beside the point. The story of Noah and the ark is not simply history. It is recounted for a purpose that is above and beyond mere historicity. That purpose will become more and more clear as the story continues.

We also see that human sin survived the flood. But remember that sin never has the last word. Remember that death was not God's plan. Remember that God makes it possible to start over – that he is the God of Second Chances. And remember that blessing hidden in the curse, for it will be the thread that ties it all together: "*And I will put enmity between you and the woman, and between your offspring and hers: he will crush your head, and you will strike his heel*" (Genesis 3:15).

Remember the Son of a woman.

3

THROUGH THE WATER

Joshua 1:1-11

FOR OVER A YEAR, my church had been engaged in a very deep Bible study on Wednesday evenings. Sometimes it seemed that we were getting bogged down because we worked fairly slowly. When we got to Luke/Acts, one of the things we learned in Luke is that certain things "had to" happen. The two on the Emmaus road were instructed by the Risen Christ that it had to happen just this way: *"Did not the Christ have to suffer...?"* (Luke 24:26). There is prophecy to fulfill. We also learned that in Acts Luke's purpose was to tell us, in many ways, that nothing can hinder God's plan. Peter learned that when he took the gospel to Cornelius, and reported to the Church, *"Who was I to think I could oppose God?"* (Acts 11:17).

We began with this: The Bible begins with a Grand Plan. The Sovereign God has a plan. It began with creation. John Walton calls Genesis 1 a temple narrative.[2] God built a temple, and then placed his "image" in it (Genesis 1:26-27). It was God's very breath that animated man, created to be the image of God (Genesis 2:7). Commanded to care for the temple, that garden of paradise, the man and his wife instead chose self over service, chose knowledge over wisdom, chose independence over freedom (and they are not the same!), and ultimately brought sin and death into God's good creation.

We learned in the previous chapter that sin has consequences, and that it grows. We learned that the image of God in man was corrupted, so that Adam's son was in Adam's image (Genesis 5:1-3) and the *imago dei*, the image of God, was lost. So many people today want to believe that they are created in the image of God. Sorry. Whatever was there became *"only evil all the time"* (Genesis 6:5) – the image of God was lost, defaced, disfigured, and corrupted.

We learned also that sin would not have the last word and that God would begin again – with a man named Comfort (Noah), a man who was *blameless among the people of his time* and who *walked with God* (Genesis 6:9), a man who would be a new Adam. For God is a God of New Beginnings and Second Chances. God sent a great flood and started over again with a new promise, a new covenant, signed and sealed with his signature – a rainbow. The Grand Plan would still go forward, unhindered by a corrupt humanity. And it would

---

[2] John H. Walton, *The Lost World of Genesis One* (Downers Grove: InterVarsity Press, 2009)

go forward because... (and here is a second attribute of God)... *God is love* (1 John 4:8b).

That's where we stopped. God rescued his good creation through the great flood. But, the Scripture tells us, the die was cast. Even as God smelled the pleasant aroma of Noah's sacrifice, he said, *"Never again will I curse the ground because of man, even though **every inclination of his heart is evil from childhood**"* (Genesis 8:21). You see, God knows what we are. And God knows that you can't change the inside simply by changing the outside. Even though the world had changed, the heart of man had not.

God began to work through one of Noah's descendants, a Chaldaean gentleman by the name of Terah. Terah moved his family away from the comforts of home and away from the diversions of the city because he had heard a Voice. His son, Abram, later to be called Abraham, continued Terah's journey, following the Voice and settling in a strange land on the strength of a promise.

It was a rather strange promise – the promise of many descendants to a childless man with a barren wife. He was bewildered; she laughed at the ridiculousness of it all. But the promise to a childless man echoed the hidden blessing from the Garden. Where Genesis 3:15 had promised that the seed of a woman would crush the tempter's head, the Covenant with Abraham promises this: *"I will make you into a great nation and I will bless you;... and all peoples on earth will be blessed through you"* (Genesis 12:2-3).

Miraculously, at the age of 100, Abraham and his 90-year-old wife, Sarah, did have a son – the son of the promise – whom they named Laughter, to remember that they had laughed at God's promise, to remind them that God is a promise-keeping God, who does not forget his promises, and who does not waver in his plans, a God for whom nothing is impossible (Genesis 18:14).

Laughter (Isaac) had two children: Red Earth (Esau) and Deceiver (Jacob). And then Jacob had children of his own – twelve of them; only one though, whom he really loved, named Joseph (Genesis 37:3).

Because it was quite obvious that their father loved their little brother more than they, the ten older brothers hated Joseph. In fact, their hatred was so strong that the writer of Genesis mentions it three times: Because of their fathers favoritism, Joseph's brothers *hated him and could not speak a kind word to him* (Genesis 37:4). After a dream of dominance, *they hated him all the more* (Genesis 37:8). After a second dream of dominance, they *were jealous of him* (Genesis 37:11) and plotted to kill him (Genesis 37:18-20).

Make a mental note of a wondrous fact: God can use even our hatred, our jealousy, and our sin to accomplish his purposes. Our failures do not stand in God's way. Even our rebellion does not hinder God's plan. Had Joseph's brothers not hated him and plotted to kill him, they would likely not have sold him into slavery. Had Joseph not been sold into slavery, his faithfulness and trust in God would not have been on display in Potiphar's household, in an Egyptian royal prison, or in Pharaoh's own court. The brothers did not recognize, all those years later in the depths of famine when they came to beg food, their own brother, the second-most powerful man in Egypt. And Joseph, whom they sought to kill, became their savior.

Joseph was able, with the Pharaoh's blessing, to move his family to a fertile plain in Egypt where they lived happily ever after – until Jacob died and the brothers feared Joseph's vengeance. Reflecting on his journey from hated little brother to falsely-accused slave to forgotten prisoner to his position of power and prestige, Joseph saw God's hand in it all. *"You intended to harm me,"* he told his frightened brothers, *"but God intended it for good to accomplish what is now being done, the saving of many lives"* (Genesis 50:20). And here's another thing you need to know: God's plan is always a plan of salvation, even if we wind up falsely accused in a prison cell.

Jump forward with me four-hundred years. Joseph was long gone, his bones in an ossuary (bone box) awaiting their return to the Land of Promise, the land of Abraham, Isaac, and Jacob (whom God renamed Israel). The Pharaoh who knew Joseph was also long gone, and the current ruler knew nothing but fear and jealousy. The good land of Goshen where Jacob's family had settled made it possible for them to prosper, and they had indeed grown into a great nation. Fearing that the *Habiru* (wanderers–Hebrews) had grown too numerous and too strong and posed a significant threat to his power, the Pharaoh made them slaves, subjected them to the whip, starvation and hard labor. He ordered the execution of any baby boy born to the descendants of Israel (Jacob). One baby boy stands out among the many who survived.

We need to pause here just a moment. The title for this chapter is "Through the Water." Please keep that in mind, for it begins here. Lutheran pastor and author Frank Honeycutt says, "When considering a river anywhere in the Bible... a Christian might think of baptism."[3] The water is important. Remember that Noah was saved through the flood. And now a little Hebrew boy is drawn from the river. We'll never know what his parents would have named him. They kept the letter of the law (but not the spirit of it) by placing their infant in a basket and floating him among the reeds along the banks of the river Nile. In that sense only, the child was "executed" by being "fed to the crocodiles." The daughter of Pharaoh found the child, felt compassion, rescued the child and named him *Moses*, "drawn from the water".[4]

In what seems an unlikely twist of fate, the princess turned to the infant's own Israelite mother as nurse for her baby. Then when he was weaned, the princess whisked him off to the palace to become a proper Egyptian prince. Moses nevertheless found himself strangely drawn to the plight of Hebrew slaves. Some stirring in his own blood perhaps led him to murder on their behalf. Forty years later, the one-time fugitive encountered God at a burning

---

[3] Frank G. Honeycutt, *Marry a Pregnant Virgin* (Minneapolis: Augsburg Fortress, 2008), p. 241

[4] Thomas Cahill, *The Gifts of the Jews* (New York: Anchor Books, 1998), p. 129. The greatest hero of Israel is an Egyptian prince with an Egyptian name.

bush, and over his heart-felt protest, found him-self confronting the Pharaoh, his adoptive brother, in a fool's quest to free a nation of slaves. But they were God's people, descendants of Abraham and heirs of the promise. God heard their cries and sent Moses to set them free (Exodus 2:24).

Moses was a reluctant "hero". Perhaps he feared that his crime would catch up with him. He did not want to obey God. He tried several times to come up with a good excuse to not obey. He tried to convince God that someone else would be a better spokesman. It's worth noting that God does not always choose the strong and bold; God often chooses the fearful and timid, the unlikely, to carry out his work.

It was not easy, and it was not quick. Real freedom seldom is. We read the story and condense time so we don't truly understand the struggle. Moses' confrontation with the Pharaoh may have lasted over several months or more. Moses begged. Pharaoh refused. God plagued. Pharaoh grew hard. Finally, through the death of his first-born, Pharaoh relented and sent Israel away. A sacrificial lamb, blood on the doorposts, and unleavened bread pointed the way to freedom and salvation, and Israel walked free – into the wilderness. The Passover event is a crucial part of the story, and deserves much fuller treatment than I can give here. But remember the death of the first-born. Remember the sacrificial lamb, the blood and the bread. They are vital to the story.

Israel came to a barrier, the Red Sea. And they arrived just about the time Pharaoh had one of those "what have I done?" moments. He'd ruined his economy by setting his slaves free. He sent his army to bring them back. And there is Moses, and a rag-tag throng of slaves, trapped "between the devil and the deep blue sea." Slavery or death seemed the only options. But God opened the way. Moses, drawn from the water, was to lead Israel through the water – through the waters of death to freedom and salvation on the other side.

I notice that the waters of the Red Sea parted when God caused a *wind* to blow. God *spoke* creation and *breathed* life into man; Jesus *spoke* healing and resurrection; the Holy Spirit *breathed* the birth of the Church at Pentecost. We have only felt the wind of God's breath; what must be the real power of God!

Fast forward with me another forty years. It is interesting that Moses lived in the desert for forty years before returning to Egypt, and now, because of their refusal to go forward and possess the promise, God condemned Israel to live in the desert for forty years until the rebels died. And then Moses also died. But God had not left them without a leader. Moses had trained a young soldier to take his place. We meet him as Moses' attendant, watching at the door while Moses prayed, learning faith by watching a faithful leader. We meet him again as a young spy, sent with eleven others to check out the land of promise. Ten came back, "We can't do it." Two came back, "We can't, but God can." Those two: Caleb, feisty and eager even in old age, who followed God *wholeheartedly*, and Joshua (Joshua 14:6-15).

Moses had reminded them, *"During the forty years that I led you through the desert, your clothes did not wear out, nor did the sandals on your feet. You ate no bread* (only manna from God) *and drank no wine* (only water from a rock)... *so that you might know that I am the LORD your God"* (Deuteronomy 29:5-6). They had been *carried on eagles' wings* as God's treasure (Exodus 19:4-6). And now they stand at another river. And their leader is a man named "Savior" (Joshua). All they have to do is cross the river and take possession of what God has promised them.

Some don't want to cross the river. They have found cities to live in, pastures for their flocks, safety for their children. They are content to stay. Some are afraid to cross. Fortified cities and well-trained soldiers wait in ambush. It is a strange place and their future is unknown and uncertain. But God didn't bring them out of Egypt to live in the desert.

There is an interesting philosophy today, something along the lines of, "Don't worry about the destination; just enjoy the journey." A t-shirt proclaims, "It's not the destination; it's the journey." I read a quote: "Who knows where life will take you, the road is long and in the end the journey is the destination." Cain had been destined to be a *restless wanderer* (Genesis 4:12), but Israel was given a destination. The wandering was punishment; the journey was supposed to end. God did not lead Israel out of Egypt to wander in the wilderness. God led them out because he had a place for them to go. They were led *out* so they could be led *in*. They could not remain slaves in Egypt and be free in the land of promise. They could not remain wilderness wanderers and settle the land

34

of blessing. The journey has a destination. The wandering must come to an end.

And now they stand at the side of the river, the promise is in sight. Joshua must lead them across one more river, the Jordan. The priests take up the Ark of Covenant on their shoulders, and walk toward the river. All eyes are on them. We must note that this is an "all or nothing" proposition. They cannot wade gently in. No "step of faith" here; it is a leap of faith. There is a steep bank and a river at flood-stage. They must jump from the riverbank into the flood. But God has promised a land, a future, a blessing. All they have to do is leave the safety of the shore and go forward into the water. And all Israel has to do is follow. All we have to do is follow our Joshua across our Jordan River. But it means leaving Egypt behind, once and for all. And it means leaving the wilderness behind, once and for all. It means *forgetting what is behind and straining toward what is ahead (and pressing) on toward the goal to win the prize for which God has called me...* (Philippians 3:14). The Promised Land awaits. The New Beginning awaits.

4

INTO THE FIRE

Nehemiah 7:73b–8:12

ONE OF THE MOST precious truths of all is this: God is a God of New Beginnings, a God of Second Chances. We learned that in the story of Noah (Comfort), a righteous man whom God used to start over after Adam's race blew it. We learned that in the last chapter as we traveled from Joseph's slavery to the Israel on the banks of the Jordan.

Freed slaves rebelled and wanted to go back to their slavery. It turned out that you could take a slave out of Egypt, but you couldn't take Egypt out of the slave. Earlier in the journey, at the very doorstep of their destination, they balked, afraid of God's good future for them. Ten of twelve spies reported, "It's a good land, but there are giants, fortified cities, and well-equipped armies. We can't take the land." Two of the twelve reported, "It's a good land, and there are giants, fortified cities, and well-equipped armies. We can't take the land, but God will give it to us" (Numbers 13). The majority isn't always right. The majority is often faithless. On the strength of a majority report, Israel turned back, condemned by God to wander in the wilderness for forty years (Numbers 14), as it turns out, one year for every day the spies spent in the Land of Promise (Numbers 13:25); condemned by God to wander aimlessly, homeless, until all the malcontents had died out. Everyone over the age of 20 would perish except two – the two faithful spies. Even Moses would not live to "possess the Promise" (Deuteronomy 32:48-52; 34:1-8).

So, after forty years wandering in the desert, we find them standing on the banks of the Jordan, the priests with the Ark of the Covenant on their shoulders about to step in so that Israel might at last take possession of the Land God had promised them. As the priests prepared to cross the river, Joshua charged the leaders of the tribes to gather stones from the river bed to build a memorial altar to remind them that God had brought them through the water safely on dry ground. Through the waters of the Red Sea, they were baptized into freedom and died to slavery. Through the waters of the Jordan, they were baptized into a new life and died to the wilderness.

It took them some years, some battles, some hardship, but they did eventually conquer the land and live productively in it. They lived under divinely-guided judges. Much of the time they seem to have had peace. But they were surrounded by enemies. Whenever they strayed from their commitment to God, whenever they failed, God sent one of those enemies as a "punishment" for sin. The enemies had strange names – Philistines (from whom we get the name *Palestine*), Midianites, Ammonites, Phoenicians. Some of the judges we remember easily–Samson, Deborah, Gideon; others are not so memorable–Caleb's little brother, Othniel; left-handed Ehud: Tola; Jair; and Jephthah, son of a prostitute. And finally, Samuel, of whom Israel demanded a king, so they could be just like everybody else.

There's a problem with that: God never intended for Israel to be just like everybody else. He set them apart. He chose them for a special place in the world. After leaving Egypt and crossing the sea, Moses led them to the foot of a mountain, called Sinai, or Horeb ("ruin"). When Moses went up the mountain, God told him to speak these words to Israel: *"You yourselves have seen what I did to Egypt, and how I carried you on eagles' wings and brought you to myself. Now if you obey me fully and keep my covenant, then out of all nations you will be my treasured possession. Although the whole earth is mine, you will be for me a kingdom of priests and a holy nation"* (Exodus 19:4-6). A kingdom of priests – to represent God to the nations and the nations to God; to intercede for the peoples of the earth; to be a vessel of grace; to be the mediator of salvation – a high and privileged calling: to be God's own treasure. They were not to be like anyone else. Their laws are priestly laws; their clothing was priestly clothing; their diet was a priestly diet; they were to be a nation of priests.

But they wanted to be just like everyone else. They were always following the gods of other nations – the fertility gods of Canaan, the storm gods, the angry and vengeful gods, Chemosh,

Dagon, and Molech, who demanded the sacrifice of children. They were also not to intermarry with the surrounding peoples, but not for the sake of any sort of racial purity.

There have been those, who read into God's prohibition on intermarriage a racial component. But there is nothing racial here. These are all Semitic peoples–Israel, Canaan, Midian and Edom were all descendants of Abraham. They are, in effect, cousins. And contrary to our sad history, this has nothing whatsoever to do with race. It is simply not a Black and White issue. There is, in fact, no Scriptural prohibition on "interracial" marriage. I put that in quotes because, also a fact, there is no "racial" issue in the Bible at all. Race is a construct of evolutionary theory and has no basis in the Bible. As such, it should never be an issue for Christians (or Jews). To divide and treat people differently, prejudicially, because of skin color or any other so-called "racial" feature is, to put it simply, sinful.

The prohibition is rather for the sake of their position as priests of God, because they were to be a holy nation, set apart to serve the Living God. They were not to intermarry, because they would then bring the idols into their homes along with their Canaanite wives and husbands. And God links idolatry and adultery as the same sort of faithlessness, the same sort of sin – the abandonment of the covenant.

But they wanted to be just like everyone else, and everybody else had kings, not judges, not priests. They demanded a king. Samuel tried to warn them–kings will tax you, kings will take your daughters as servants and your sons as soldiers, kings will take your crops, kings will make you slaves. But the people wouldn't listen. God told Samuel to give them what they asked, and a "new beginning" was set in motion.

Their first king, Saul, turned out to be no great prize. Their second, David, for all his faults and failures, was at least willing and eager to repent. And, in response to his heart's desire for God, God made a new covenant with David stating that there would always be a son of David as king (2 Samuel 7, esp. vv. 11-16). God repeated the covenant to David's son, Solomon (1 Kings 9:3-9, esp. v. 8). After Solomon died, the kingdom divided because of his son's refusal to listen to the advice of the elders (1 Kings 12). They urged him to lighten the tax burden Solomon had imposed. Rehoboam refused, pledging to be a harsher ruler than his father had been. Israel, the northern ten tribes, was ruled by Jeroboam, son of Nebat, not a descendant of David. Israel continued to be ruled by Jeroboam's descendants – some good, some evil. God sent prophets – Amos, Hosea, and Micah, the latter prophesying in Judah, but with a sidelong glance at Israel, as if to say, "This word is for you, too. Please listen and learn." Israel's kings did not listen and the Assyrian Empire overran them, dispersing them to the winds, when the capital city of Samaria was destroyed in 721 BC. Assyrian conquest was designed to obliterate their enemies, and so Israel ceased to exist as all ten northern tribes were made extinct.

Descendants of King David and King Solomon continued to rule the Southern Kingdom, comprised of the tribes of Judah (from which we get "Jew) and Benjamin. Some of the Judean kings, like their northern cousin were good and some were bad.. We are treated to accounts where some are excused as not as bad as their fathers; and some, we are told, were not as good as they might have been. God sent prophets to them, too, most notably Isaiah, Jeremiah, and Ezekiel, to call king and people to repentance. But they were not willing. Even the tirades of Jeremiah, the object lessons of Ezekiel, the bright promises of Isaiah, and the not-so-gentle urgings of Habakkuk, Haggai and Zephaniah were not enough. They would be good – as scolded children are good for awhile and then fall back into their old ways.

God raised up non-writing prophets like Elijah and Elisha. The people, and their kings, preferred the fertility gods, the angry gods of wood and stone, the Baals and the Asherah poles, the high places and the groves where they could indulge in the same sensual "worship" as their pagan neighbors. They had long forgotten that they were to be a *kingdom of priests and a holy nation* (Exodus 19:6).

Babylon appeared on the horizon. Assyria had defeated and destroyed Israel, and had come knocking on the very doors of Jerusalem, when, in 701 BC, Babylonian armies attacked the Assyrian capital of Nineveh. The Assyrians abandoned their dream of conquest in their rush to protect their capital. "The enemy of my enemy is my friend," says a Middle Eastern proverb, and Judah's King Hezekiah welcomed the savior Babylonians. To show them he was their friend, Hezekiah opened up his armory and his treasury to show off. Even nature seemed to be against Assyria. In 607 BC, the Tigris River flooded, washing away part of Nineveh's great wall, and the Babylonians swept in and took over.

The savior became the enemy, and just two years after the defeat of Nineveh, Nebuchadnezzar, the powerful soldier/emperor of Babylonia, laid siege to Jerusalem and began deporting her finest young men. Their failure to listen to their prophets, their continuing and worsening idolatry, their abandonment of any real worship of God, led to God withdrawing his protection. *The wages of sin is death* (Romans 6:23). Sin always has consequences.

Four young men, tall, handsome, intelligent, were in that first contingent of exiles. Hananiah, Azariah, Mishael, and Daniel – to be given the Babylonian names of Shadrach, Meshach, Abed-nego, and Belteshazzar, stood strong in the face of persecution. Twenty years after their exile, Nebuchadnezzar's army defeated and destroyed Jerusalem. A nation in mourning watched their beautiful temple looted, burned, and torn down. That golden temple, the House of God, where the Glorious Presence of God had come with fire on the altar (2 Chronicles 7:1-3), became a burning heap of rubble. Judah, the remnant of Israel, walked forlornly toward Babylon into exile, many of them never to return. They would settle in ghettos, make homes, build families, and somehow survive.

With the temple gone and the priesthood disbanded, they would gather in synagogues to read their Scriptures and be taught by rabbis. They would retain whatever of their faith they could.

They would repent over and over. They would pray and dream of home.

A brief detour: God's Glorious Presence, the *shekinah*, is depicted in the scripture as fire. It was a pillar of fire that protected the wilderness wanderers (Exodus 13:21). It was with a continual fire on the altar that Israel was to remember God's presence (Leviticus 6:8-13). God answered David's cry for forgiveness at the threshing floor of Araunah with fire from heaven (1 Chronicles 21:26); showed his presence in Solomon's temple by consuming the sacrifice with fire from heaven (2 Chronicles 7:1); answered Elijah's challenge to Jezebel's Baalite priests with fire from heaven (1 Kings 18:16-42); and thwarted Samaria's attempt to capture Elijah with fire from heaven (2 Kings 1). God, it seems, is no stranger to fire. Fire is his servant.

But fire has another purpose – it purifies. It burns away impurities. It burns off the dross so that pure gold might appear. That's what Malachi says in his predictions of the appearing of the Messiah – *"He will be like a refiners fire or a launderer's soap. He will sit as a refiner and purifier of silver... Then the LORD will have men who will bring offerings in righteousness"* (Malachi 3:2-3).

One such event stands as a metaphor for the exile and a call for Israel to remember her God. It happened to three of those four young men I mentioned.

Nebuchadnezzar had a very high opinion of himself. To gain favor, his officials were constantly stroking his ego, telling him how wonderful he was, what a genius, how handsome and how he had been favored by their gods as the most powerful and wealthiest ruler in history. They convinced him to build a giant statue of himself, to set it up in the town square, and proclaim a day of worship (Daniel 3). He, the imperial Nebuchadnezzar, ruler of the world, was to be the god of Babylon. Regal music would fill the air, and everyone would bow with their faces to the ground and worship him.

The day came, the golden statue gleamed in the sunlight, and the crowds gathered as ordered. All the royal officials were there. The atmosphere was electric with excitement and celebration. The trumpets sounded and, as one man, the entire crowd knelt with their faces to the ground. Nebuchadnezzar, on his resplendent throne, beamed with pride... until his eyes fell on three men standing proudly erect. They did not bow. The king frowned and ordered the trumpets to sound again just in case the men misunderstood. They did not move – they did not so much as tip their heads.

Enraged, Nebuchadnezzar called them forward. "Bow or else." The penalty was death by burning, and the furnace was ready just in case anyone should defy the king's order. The trumpets sounded again, and again the three refused to bow. Their answer to the king was simple, *"Our God is able to deliver us, and he will rescue us. But, even if he does not, we want you to know that we will not serve your gods or worship your images"* (Daniel 3:16-18).

They were thrown into the fire, but, to the king's astonishment, they did not die. Instead, they were up, walking unbound, joined by and conversing with a fourth man, one the king described as being *"like a son of the gods"* (Daniel 3:25). They were delivered, safe and sound, without even the odor of fire on them.

A powerful image to the exiles – their God would deliver them. He had not abandoned them. Their exile was a trial by fire, a time of purification and focus. More than that, their messiah was sure to come. The "fourth man" was with them already. This prophetic glimpse was a promise, but who would be the "fourth man"?

Almost seventy years after those first exiles left their homes in Jerusalem, a new emperor sent the first group of exiles back to Jerusalem to begin the rebuilding of the temple of God. Eighty years later Ezra the priest returned to Jerusalem, followed a decade later by Nehemiah, and Israel began the long trek home, a chastened people of God.

God is still the God of Second Chances. He had purified them with fire, his *treasured possession*, and was ready to begin once more to build *a kingdom of priests and a holy nation*. And that is still God's plan. But, would they be ready? Would they be faithful? Would they live as the purified people of God? The God of New Beginnings was giving them another chance.

5

IN THE BEGINNING, PART 2

John 1:1-18

"Ask a high school or college student about cheating, and before you can finish the sentence, the person will blurt out two things: 'Everybody does it,' and 'It's no big deal.'"[5]

According to a PricewaterhouseCooper's study of consumer attitudes toward piracy conducted in 2011, "54 percent 'felt that everyone was doing it,' and 57 percent actually had a friend or family member recommend unlicensed content. Of course, this isn't statistical proof that everyone actually is pirating content, but this kind of perception may well become a self-fulfilling prophecy.

---

[5] Regan McMahon, "Everybody Does It", September 6, 2007, (http://www.sfgate.com/education/article/Everybody-Does-It-2523376.php)

If everyone believes that everyone is doing it, then everyone may as well be doing it themselves."[6]

We learned in the last chapter that Israel wanted a king because they wanted to be just like everyone else. And in being like everyone else, they forfeited the uniqueness that God desired for them. They were not supposed to be just like everyone else. God's plan for Israel was that they be his *treasured possession*, a *kingdom of priests and a holy nation* (Exodus 19:4-6). Their laws were priestly laws; their diet was a priestly diet; their clothing was priestly clothing. They, however, chose to follow the world, to worship the idols. They maintained their tradition of the worship of God, but their hearts weren't in it. We learn from Jeremiah that they thought God would never punish them. They were the "chosen", which, to their way of thinking, meant that they could pretty much do as they pleased without consequences. There are people like that today, claiming that "God loves me just the way I am." The implication of course, is that God is okay with sin, that we don't need repentance, salvation, or transformation. We're just okay the way we are. God loves us and won't mind if we live however we wish.

This is an unhealthy view of "election" that allows one to "sin every day in word, thought, and deed" without consequences. If one is among the "elect", their sin does not matter, they think. It has been expressed as, "God has forgiven me of all sin

---

[6] Janko Roettgers, "Piracy: Everybody Does It; Everything Should Be Free", Feb. 16, 2011, (http://gigaom.com/2011/02/16/piracy-consumer-attitudes/)

– past, present and future." A man asked his pastor if God would forgive him for a sin he planned for the next day. The pastor responded, "If you know it's sin, why do you plan to do it?" A man standing in the foyer of a church said, "I sin every day in word, thought, and deed." The pastor looked him in the eye and asked, "Why?" This sort of Gnostic[7] dualism rears its ugly head in the church – the body is sinful and sin is unavoidable; the spirit is what matters. This is also part of the ancient Manichaean[8] heresy that both St. Augustine and his opponent Pelagius rejected. Sin is a matter of the will, of the soul. Physical matter has no moral nature and sin cannot be imputed to the body anymore than to a rock or a tree. Sin is always a spiritual issue even when it involves the physical body. We cannot excuse sin as either inevitable or unavoidable.

---

[7] Gnosticism is a the belief that salvation comes through knowledge (from the Greek *gnosis*–knowledge), but the knowledge is hidden from the average person and only available through special enlightenment. The Gospel of Judas and other "lost gospels" were gnostic writings. Those "lost" writings, including the Nag Hammadi codices, were the basis for Dan Brown's fiction *The DaVinci Code*. Gnosticism appeared in many forms, but one basic doctrine was that matter was evil, created by an evil demiurge (lower power), while spirit was good, created by God. Wisdom (Sophia) is the highest good.

[8] Manichaeism is a Third Century heresy that arose in Persia. It held the same dualism between spirit (good) and matter (evil) that characterized Gnosticism. St. Augustine subscribed to a Manichaean philosophy before he became a Christian.

Many modern Christians, though, just like the ancient Judeans, think that their "election", their chosen-ness, exempts them from the consequences of sin. As Judah rejected Jeremiah's calls to repentance and prophecies of judgment ("We are God's chosen people. We have the Temple, God's dwelling place, in our midst. God would never destroy us."), so many Christians today place the same claim on their "election." We would do well to listen closely to the old prophets.

The result of that sort of thinking, of course, as with any parent worth his salt, would be punishment. If my kids took that attitude toward me, they'd face consequences. Sin always has consequences. The result of that sort of thinking for Israel was destruction by the Assyrian Empire; the result for Judah was Babylonian exile. But God is a God of Second Chances; a God of New Beginnings. We left the story last chapter as the exiles began to return home under the leadership of Ezra and Nehemiah. They had a chance to start over. As Ezra read the Law, the people grieved and repented and pledged to obey God. Nehemiah declared it a holy day, a feast day, *"for the joy of the LORD is your strength"* (Nehemiah 8:10). If they would, they could once again be *a kingdom of priests and a holy nation.*

It turns out they couldn't, or wouldn't. They got discouraged building the temple, and Habakkuk had to call them back. They got discouraged with the effort of worship, and Malachi tried to call them back. Malachi's audience considered it a burden to worship (1:13), and their priests weren't much better – choosing rather to cater to the perverted

49

desires of the people for entertainment and easy religion rather than to speak God's truth into their lives. Malachi fairly shouts at the priests, *"The lips of a priest ought to preserve knowledge, and from his mouth men should seek instruction – because he is the messenger of the LORD (2:7) (but instead) you cause many to stumble..."* They considered worship an exercise in futility. Malachi brings God's charge: *"You have said it is futile to serve God. What did we gain by carrying out his requirements..."* (3:14).

You see, as we read in Leviticus, if worship is to be meaningful it must be purposeful. True worship is never accidental. We don't just stumble into it. We prepare. And the Levitical ceremonies of preparation, washing, dressing, sacrifices, were an indication of how seriously they took worship of God.

We don't accidentally tithe – we plan and prepare. We "dress" for worship, at least figuratively, by preparing our hearts for the moment we walk through the doors. Malachi's issue, contrary to a lot of modern preaching, was not the matter of tithing. Their lack of tithing was a symptom of a deeper failure. It went hand in hand with bringing blemished sacrifices, left-overs, and cast-offs. They were offering diseased animals in sacrifice. They wanted to keep the best, improve their herds, and had to find a way to get rid of the lame, blind, and diseased animals. They offered to God what they would never offer to the governor. That's not sacrifice; that's disposal. The sacrifice was a symptom. The same is true today. Tithing is not a money issue (as many people think); it is a heart issue. We don't take worship seriously; we don't

take grace seriously; we don't take salvation seriously; we don't take God seriously. We approach
God in the off-handed way we approach much of
the rest of our lives. We tip our hats to God once a
week, drop a dollar or ten in the offering, and call
it good – we've done our duty.

God doesn't want our duty; he wants our heart.
He doesn't want our sacrifices; he wants our devotion. The judge Samuel had instructed King Saul
to destroy everything and everyone following a
battle with the Amalekites. *But Saul and the people
spared Agag, and the best of the sheep, and of the oxen,
and of the fatlings, and the lambs, and all that was good,
and would not utterly destroy them* (1 Samuel 15:9).
When Samuel confronted Saul about his disobedience, the king claimed that he had saved the best
for a sacrifice to God. Samuel responded, *"Hath
the LORD as great delight in burnt offerings and sacrifices, as in obeying the voice of the LORD? Behold,
to obey is better than sacrifice, and to hearken than
the fat of rams"* (1 Samuel 15:22, KJV). As a child,
I would hear those word from my mother whenever I would bring her a handful of dandelions as
a peace offering after my failure to obey.

Such disobedience can come back to haunt us.
Saul chose to spare King Agag. It was his descendant, Haman the Agagite, who was Judah's mortal
enemy in the story of Esther. The disobedience
we attempt to excuse may turn out to be our ultimate destruction. But for Esther's courage and
Mordecai's insistence–and God's grace–Saul's sin
might have resulted in the destruction of his nation.

Failure to tithe, or refusal to tithe, is a symptom
of an ungrateful heart, a sign that we do not honor

God. My point is not the tithe, as Malachi's point was not the tithe – but a heart devoted to God. Worship is not in form and appearance, but true worship is *in spirit and in truth* (John 4:24). Isaiah had said it 400 years earlier, *"These people come near to me with their mouth and honor me with their lips, but their hearts are far from me"* (Isaiah 29:13). Malachi told the returned exiles that they remain under the curse, *"because you have not set your heart to honor me"* (Malachi 2:2). Worship cannot be in form and function, but must come from a heart for God. Your heart is what matters. Where have you set your heart?

So even at home in Israel, the exile continued. The Bible doesn't give us the details of the intervening years, what we call "The Inter-testamental Period", so we must turn to secular history to fill in the gaps.

The people were under the thumb of the Persian Empire until Alexander the Great rolled through in 325 BC. After just seven years, he died and his Greek Empire was divided between four of his generals – two of whom fought over Israel: the Syrian Seleucids and the Egyptian Ptolemies, with Israel as the knot in the tug-of-war rope between them. Eventually the Seleucids dominated and to ensure their control, Antiochus IV Epiphanes, declared the Hebrew language illegal. Seventy Jewish scholars carefully translated their Scriptures from Hebrew into Greek, giving Israel the Septuagint. Antiochus also banned Jewish Temple worship, circumcision, and festival observance. In 167 BC, Antiochus Epiphanes desecrated the Jerusalem temple, set up an altar to Zeus and sacrificed swine in the temple. Daniel 11 appears to refer rather specifically to the Greek Empire, it's division, the desecration of the temple and the *"abomination that causes desolation"* by a king who *"will exalt and magnify himself above every god and will say unheard of things against the God of gods"* (Daniel 11, esp. vv 11, 36).

This fulfillment of Daniel's prophecy inflamed Jewish passions, and was the spark that lit the Maccabean Revolt. Judah the Hammer (Maccabaeus) led his brothers and other like-minded rebels in a guerilla war against the Syrian forces. In 165 BC, they prevailed, recaptured the temple, cleansed it, and under priestly leadership, lit the menorah and rededicated the temple. They filled the menorah with all the sacred oil they could find, about a day's worth, and miraculously it burned for eight days. Jews today continue to celebrate the eight-day Feast of the Dedication, Hanukkah.

But it was a political victory, not a spiritual one. The Seleucids continued their somewhat muted control until 140 BC.

With Seleucid tolerance, the Hasmonean kingdom was set up and friendship with the Republic of Rome was established. That lasted just about 70 years, until General Pompey decided that "friendship" was really an invitation for conquest. In 63 BC, Pompey attacked Jerusalem and set it under the control of a Roman consul. For services rendered to Julius Caesar and a considerable bribe, Julius appointed an ambitious Idumean, Antipater, as administrator of Judea. In 47 BC, Antipater's son Herod, was made governor of Galilee. After a complex series of political maneuvers, Herod was appointed "King of the Jews" in 37 BC. He is known today as Herod the Great. His childhood friend, Gaius Octavius, became Caesar in 31 BC and was given the title Augustus in 27 BC.

Now the stage was set. With foreign domination experienced daily with an occupation army and a phony king, the stage was indeed set. Remember the story of Jacob and Esau? These are the descendants of Jacob being ruled by a descendant of Esau. Worse, all the political intrigue had made their phony king delusional, paranoid, and sadistically cruel. The time was right and the climate was ripe for something to break. Messianic fever ran higher than ever. A Roman procurator was installed to keep Herod in check. Fire-brand preachers roamed the countryside stirring up rebellion with end-times prophecies.

Then, as if out of the mists, a group of foreign dignitaries appears in Jerusalem, knock on Herod's door, and ask a bewildering question: *"Where is he who is **born** king of the Jews? We have seen his star in the east and have come to do him homage"* (Matthew 2:2).

"Born king?" One can imagine Herod demanding, "BORN king? King of the Jews?" Herod's official Roman title was, "King of the Jews." Not a Jew. Not a descendant of David. But king, nonetheless. And he intended to remain king. He had murdered his favorite wife and oldest son out of a paranoid fear that they were plotting to take his kingdom from him. So he wasn't about to sit still for *this*. Matthew wryly records, *"When King Herod heard this he was disturbed, and all Jerusalem with him*" (Matthew 2:3). You bet he was disturbed, and if Herod wasn't happy, nobody was safe.

With a wink and a sly smile, Herod sent the Magi on their way to find a baby somewhere in Bethlehem, for that is what the prophet Micah had predicted (Micah 5:2). "Go, pay him homage. Then come tell me where he is so I too may pay him homage." But Herod had murder in his heart, and when the Magi did not return, Herod launched his attack.

Do you recall how Pharaoh dealt with the growing population of Hebrews in his kingdom? He ordered the death of all the baby boys? One survived to lead Israel out of slavery. One Egyptian prince, drawn from the water, led Israel to freedom. Do you know how Herod dealt with the threat of a genuine king of Israel? He ordered the death of all the baby boys in the vicinity of Bethlehem. One survived, ironically, because his parents fled to, of all places, Egypt. Joseph's brothers went to Egypt to survive the famine. Now, the descendant of one of those brothers, Judah, goes to Egypt to survive the rage of a false king. And the prophet Hosea had said, *"Out of Egypt I called my son"* (Hosea 11:1). Joseph kept his wife and her baby safe in Egypt until after Herod died, and then returned to their humble home in Nazareth of Galilee.

His wife and *her* baby. Remember the curse in the Garden, the curse with the hidden blessing? *"And I will put enmity between you and the woman,"* God told the serpent. *"And between your offspring and hers; he will crush your head, and you will strike his heel"* (Genesis 3:15). The Hebrew actually says, "Between your seed and her seed." Not the seed of a man, but of a woman. And Isaiah picks that up when he says, *"Therefore the Lord himself will give you a sign: The virgin will be with child and will give birth to a son, and will call him Immanuel"* (Isaiah 7:14).

Immanuel means "God with us". So who is this child? Or, in the words of the song,
"What child is this, who, laid to rest,
On Mary's lap is sleeping?
Whom angels greet with anthems sweet,
While shepherds watch are keeping?"[9]

The angel told Joseph to give him the name – we read it in English, so it's rendered *Jesus*. That's what we call him. But in Hebrew, it's *Yeshua*, or *Joshua*. Do you remember what the name *Joshua* means? It means "savior". Variations of the name include that of Israel's last king, Hoshea, who was taken captive by the victorious Assyrian army, and the prophet Hosea, who depicts the deep love of God by marrying and then rescuing a prostitute. There is also the high priest Joshua who figures in the prophecies of Haggai and Zechariah. But we look back to the Joshua who led Israel across the Jordan River and helped lead them to possess the Land of Promise. It was that Joshua who, in some ways, appears to pre-figure this one, the one we call Jesus. *"And you are to give him the name Jesus, because he will save his people from their sins"* (Matthew 1:21). You are to call him *Savior*.

---

[9] "What Child Is This?" words by William C. Dix (1837-1898), public domain

Who is this child? John answers in a more pro-found way. This may seem insignificant for the moment, but the "Bible" that John used was the Septuagint, produced in the reign of Antiochus IV Epiphanes. And John begins his gospel with precisely the same formulation as Genesis in the Septuagint, Ἐν αρχῆ (en arché), *In the beginning.* Compare these side by side –

Genesis 1:1 – *In the beginning* (Ἐν αρχῆ) *God created the heavens and the earth...*

John 1:1 – *In the beginning* (Ἐν αρχῆ) *was the Word, and the Word was with God, and the Word was God. He was with God in the beginning* (εν αρχῆ). *Through him all things were made...* John deliberately identifies "the Word" as the same God who cre-ated *in the beginning.*

Then John does something unexpected. This Word, this Creator God... not some remote deity; not the "hidden" God of Scripture; not "out there" somewhere... *The Word became flesh and made his dwelling among us* (John 1:14a) – literally, pitched his tent in our midst, as the tabernacle was set up in the very center of Israel's wilderness camp.

Numbers, chapter 2 gives the plan for the twelve tribes to both travel and camp. Three tribes each to the north, south, east, and west. Directly in the center of camp, the tabernacle was to be set up. When the nation was encamped, the tent of God was in the midst, in the middle, and the pillar of cloud/fire, representing the Glorious Presence, rested above the Most Holy Place, the sacred tent that housed the ark of the covenant and its sacred cover, the mercy seat with its sheltering cherubs. John's affirmation that the Word (God) made flesh pitching his tent "among us", or in our midst, is a reminder of the wilderness tabernacle. It is an affirmation that Jesus is Immanuel, God with us, just as the pillar of the Glorious Presence was with Israel.

The ancient hymn recorded in Philippians 2:5-11 tells us that Jesus, in very form (Greek: μορφε– morphé) God, put off his deity, his "God-ness", and took the form (same Greek word: μορφε) of humanity. Jesus, the Second Person of the Triune Godhead, equal to and eternal with the Father, stepped down from the throne of heaven and submitted to all the limitations of humanity, including the ultimate limitation imposed by death.

The *Word became flesh...* God became a man, took up his dwelling in his temple (Genesis 1), and, John says, *We have seen his glory, the glory of the One and Only who came from the Father, full of grace and truth* (John 1:14b). This "One and Only" is a prophet like Moses (Deuteronomy 18:15, 18). *The law was given through Moses; grace and truth came through Jesus Christ* (John 1:17).

God, the God of New Beginnings and Second Chances, did not send another Adam, another Noah, another Moses, another Joshua, or another David. He came himself, in the flesh, to be prophet, Comforter, a new Adam, son of David, born King of the Jews, Savior. The King himself has come. God himself, in the flesh, has come to deliver us from our own Egypt, from our own wilderness wandering, leading a new Israel to take possession of new Promised Land.

And it is a new beginning.

6

THROUGH THE WATER, PART 2

John 4:4-15

W E BEGAN THE LAST chapter by taking note of some similarities between Moses and Jesus. They are a little shocking, particularly if you're among the crowd that thinks the Old Testament and New Testament tell different stories, like two parallel roads that never meet, or if you're among those who think we don't need the Old Testament. We simply cannot comprehend the New Testament story without the Old Testament background – and we cannot really comprehend the Old Testament without the New to complete it. Together they tell a single, coherent story. If we continue to view the Bible as a library, a collection of sixty-six relatively unrelated books, though, it is easy to miss that great meta-narrative of God's Grand Plan.

The similarities began with the way the powers responded to the threat – Pharaoh, in response to the growing "nation" of Israelites, ordered that all the boys born to Hebrew women were to be drowned in the Nile. Herod, in response to the Magi's search for the "born king of the Jews", ordered that all the baby boys in the region of Bethlehem were to be killed. One brave mother defied Pharaoh, and her son, "Drawn from the Water" (Moses) survived to deliver Israel from Egyptian slavery. One brave family defied Herod, escaped to Egypt (of all places), and Mary's Son, "Savior" (Jesus) survived to offer himself as a savior from the powers of sin, death, and hell. Moses – out of Egypt; Jesus – out of Egypt. Both had a life mission to deliver their people, one from physical slavery, the other from slavery to sin.

The similarities don't end there.

Moses, drawn from the water, led Israel through the Red Sea away from Egypt. In the wilderness, they were hungry; God gave them a special sort of bread, which they called "manna". The Hebrew word suggests that it was something completely unknown to them, that "manna" is more a question than an answer – "What is it?" Our vernacular would be to call it "whachamacallit". The answer to the question is the promise God gave Moses, *"I will rain down bread from heaven"* (Exodus 16:4). When they were thirsty, Moses prayed and God gave them water from a rock (Exodus 17:1-7). He led them as far as the Jordan River, where Joshua took over, and after Moses' death, Joshua led them across the river to possess the promised land.

We wrote earlier about the significance of the water, as a symbol of baptism. We noted there that God took them out of Egypt because he wanted them in the Promised Land. God did not deliver

Israel from slavery so they could wander in the wilderness. There was always a destination in mind, always a planned ending to the journey. God took them out so he could take them in. They could not possess the promised land while they remained slaves in Egypt. But neither could they possess the promised land while they remained wanderers in the desert. A journey without a destination is just aimless wandering. The journey to be worth making must, at some point, come to an end. However, as we've gone through the Old Testament, as we've followed their progress – or lack thereof – we've discovered that they don't seem to have gotten the point. They were to possess the land, not merely live on it. They were to possess the land as a temple, as a sacred place, a gift from God. Moses and Joshua both warned the people not to forget God. In addition, they were to be *a kingdom of priests and a holy nation* (Exodus 19:4-6). *That* was the point. But it was not the whole point.

We also noted in an earlier chapter how they thought being God's "chosen" was a point of privilege. It's the same thing we hear these days – "God loves me just the way I am." True, but only half true. Yes, God loves you the way you are, but he loves you too much to leave you the way you are. God has a plan for you, but not just for you. God's plan for you is that you will be part of his bigger plan for the Church and for the world. God wants to include you, but for that to happen, he has to change you so that you will *reflect the Lord's glory* (2 Corinthians 3:18). Peter appropriated Exodus language and applied it to the Church: *But you are a chosen people, a royal priesthood, a holy nation, a people belonging to God, that you may declare the praises of him who called you out of darkness into his wonderful light. Once you were not a people, but now you are the people of God...* (1 Peter 2:9-10). They, and we, were not chosen for privilege, but for purpose. Their purpose was to "bless the nations" (Genesis 12:3) by bringing the Messiah to the world. Our purpose is to shine the light of Christ into a dark world, to bring good news to the world (Matthew 5:14-16; 28:18-20).

So, how do we respond to being "chosen"? How do we become "mirrors of God"? The same way Israel responded – through the water.

As I was preparing to write this chapter, I did a quick survey of how water figures in John's story of Jesus. John doesn't tell of Jesus' baptism, but Jesus did appear at the Jordan river where John was baptizing. The baptism narrative appears in Matthew 3, Mark 1, and Luke 3. But take note of this:

In John's first chapter, John declared that Jesus is the one who will baptize with the Holy Spirit (John 1:33). In chapter 2, Jesus changes water into wine. In chapter 3, he tells Nicodemus that one must be born of both water and spirit – from John's perspective that means the waters of baptism and the gift of the Holy Spirit. Nicodemus, like many today, takes it to mean physical birth and spiritual birth. In chapter 4, Jesus meets the Samaritan woman at Jacob's well, and declares to her that he can give her *living water* that will quench spiritual thirst and give eternal life. In chapter 5, Jesus heals the invalid man by the pool who felt trapped by his inability to get to the water. Jesus becomes healing water for him. In chapter 6, Jesus walks on the stormy waters of Galilee to calm the disciples and their storm. And in chapter 7, Jesus stood up at the Feast of Tabernacles, at the ritual of remembering the water from the rock in the wilderness, and calls, *"If anyone is thirsty, let him come to me and drink"* (John 7:37), along with the promise to give *streams of living water*. Then, in the ninth chapter, Jesus sends the man born blind to wash for healing in the Pool of Siloam.

More even than Moses, Jesus' ministry had to do with water. The comparisons are crucial. If Israel wanted to be free from slavery in Egypt, they had to pass through the Red Sea. There was simply no other way. If Israel wanted to possess the Promised Land, they had to pass through the Jordan River. Again, there was no other way. (Well, there was, but they'd rejected that one forty years earlier.)

In John 3, we have Jesus' encounter with Nicodemus. You may notice in the story that Jesus never answered Nicodemus initial reason for the meeting. Jesus short-circuited Nicodemus with his very first response, *"I tell you the truth..."*

"I tell you the truth" is a poor translation of the Greek. It's accurate, just not the best. In Greek, a word repeated is for emphasis. Thus, when a word appears twice, in this case the word αμην (amen – which is translated "truly", or "let it be so"), we need to double up on the meaning. A better translation would be "truly, truly", or as the KJV, "verily, verily". The way we want to understand this is: "This is a true truth" or "of all truths, this is most true." This is a kingdom absolute. Jesus is not just saying, "I'm telling you the truth", like a used car salesman, he's declaring an ultimate truth. You have to understand this point of translation because it is essential to understanding what Jesus was saying. In a world where truth is often relative, this one is a fixed star.

"Truly, truly, I tell you, no one can see the kingdom of God unless he is born again" (John 3:3). We know that some of these words have double meanings. This one, ἄνωθεν (anothen), means both "again" and "from above". This second birth is from above. How is that? Nicodemus was confused because he heard "second": "How can a man go back into his mother's womb and be born a second time?" Jesus' answer has to do with "above", that is, the kingdom of God and not with human life. *"I am telling you a truth of truths, no one can enter the kingdom of heaven unless he is born of water and the Spirit"* (John 3:5). The water, I believe (along with many Bible scholars), is a reference to baptism, a reflection (or memory) of Israel crossing the Red Sea, a symbol for the believer of leaving slavery; no longer a slave to sin, to use the language of Romans 6:16-18. For us, passing through the water symbolizes our becoming part of the new Israel, the Church.

Jesus' answer to Nicodemus question about going back to his mother's womb makes it plain that he was not talking about physical birth. It is not possible. It is not even desirable. He was, and thus we, are talking about spiritual birth. *Flesh gives birth to flesh, but the Spirit* (not just "spirit"), THE

64

Spirit *gives birth to spirit.* This is the work of the Holy Spirit in the life of one who believes in Jesus.

I think it's an interesting image. A baby does not seek to be born; it grows to the point that the birth is inevitable. And I suspect that many Christians are spiritual *caesareans*–forced to birth before they were ready. They have been argued into submission, prayed over, dragged to the altar, pounded on the back, forced to vomit up some confession of faith before they even taste the sweet milk of grace. Many altar-calls are emotionally-laden appeals, and often–more often than we might care to admit–result in catharsis rather than conversion. People rise from those altars emotionally spent but not truly converted. What faith they have is sickly and weak. A chick does not peck its way out of the shell until it is ready; but when it is ready, desperation sets in and it must be free. When the time comes, a baby must be born. It is not the altar or the evangelist or the desperately praying parent who brings spiritual birth; it is always and only the work of the Holy Spirit. And it is a timely work, easily undone by impatient evangelists.

God still desires a kingdom of priests and a holy nation. God still desires a peculiar people, who were once not a nation, but through his grace become a nation. And God is still working out his plan. Crossing the Red Sea was not the end of the journey for Israel. Baptism is not the end of the journey for us. Just as Israel had two baptisms in reaching the Land of Promise, the Red Sea and the Jordan, so we also have two baptisms on our journey to reach the Promised Kingdom. We are not simply to be delivered from sin; we are to go on and be delivered into a grand promise. So this first step is not optional. If we would participate in the working out of God's plan, Jesus says, *"You **must** be born again (from above)."* You must be born through the water. Jesus, in his baptism, led the way for us. When John the Baptist objected to baptizing Jesus – the one *who knew no sin* (2 Corinthians 5:21) did not need the baptism of repentance – Jesus said that his baptism was *"to fulfill all righteousness"* (Matthew 3:15). Just as Moses led Israel through the Red Sea, so Jesus leads the Church through the waters of baptism.

As I said, though, that is not the end of the story. It is only one step. Remember that in all of this God is the God of New Beginnings, the God of Second Chances. Not surprisingly, it happens to relate to water.

John 4 begins with Jesus engaged in baptizing. The Pharisees heard that Jesus was baptizing more disciples than John. Jesus, however, was not baptizing for repentance, but as an entry into the kingdom of God. There is a difference: John echoes the Red Sea escape from Egyptian slavery (Exodus 14); Jesus echoes the Jordan River entrance to the Land of Promise (Joshua 3); John echoes Moses; Jesus echoes Joshua. Jesus heard that the Pharisees were concerned, so, John says, he headed back to Galilee, out of the reach of the Jerusalem crowd. But to get there by the short road, he had to pass through the region of Samaria. He stopped at Jacob's Well to rest and sent the disciples on ahead to buy lunch. That's when a Samaritan woman stopped by to draw water.

There is a lot more to this story but we need to skip over the usual and focus on the water rather than the woman. You have heard the saying, "water, water everywhere, but nary a drop to drink"? That was Jesus' predicament. He was sitting by the well, but with no way to draw water. So when the woman arrived, Jesus asked her if she would give him a drink. The woman is the one who brings up the cultural taboo – that Jews don't associate with Samaritans and that men don't converse with strange women, and that in asking her for water, Jesus was violating both. Jesus redirects her attention.

"If you knew the gift of God and who it is who asks you for a drink, you would have asked him and he would have given you living water" (John 4:10).

First, the "gift of God". The idea of these words is that this is a "free gift", no strings attached, free for the asking. It is also a regal gift, the endowment of a king or rich man. The same word is used for the gift of the Spirit in the book of Acts.[10] In other words, if she'd known who Jesus was, she'd have done the asking and he the giving. But what would "the gift of God" be giving? Not just water from Jacob's Well, but "living water." What is that?

Just like Nicodemus, this poor woman was confused. She looked at Jesus and then into the well. It was deep and he had no bucket, so... how might this work? For some people, "living water" is that which is flowing, comes from a spring, in a creek or river. Some churches don't use baptisteries;

---

[10] Joseph H. Mayfield, "John", *Beacon Bible Commentary* (Kansas City: Beacon Hill Press of Kansas City, 1965), 7:65

they only baptize in "living water." But they're still stuck on natural water, H_2O. It doesn't really appear that Jesus is talking about what the woman thinks he is. And he says as much. In fact, Jesus is not talking about H_2O at all but about something else.

"No, whoever drinks from this well will be thirsty again. But whoever drinks the water I give him will never thirst. Indeed, the water I give him will become in him a spring of water welling up to eternal life" (John 4:13-14).

The Psalmist saw a vision of the way God treats the righteous: *"you give them drink from your river of delights"* (Psalm 36:8). In Psalm 46, that begins, *"God is our refuge and strength,"* the Psalmist sings, *"There is a river whose streams make glad the city of God, the holy place where the Most High dwells"* (Psalm 46:4). In the coming kingdom, God says, *"I will extend peace to her like a river..."* (Isaiah 66:12). Remember the river. We're not there yet, but it's an important part of the conclusion. It is, as Jesus said, a river of life, water that springs up to eternal life.

One more glance and we must close this chapter. The Feast of Tabernacles comes, when Israel remembers the wilderness, living in tents, eating manna, drinking water that flows out of a rock. In that festival, there is a ritual where water is "wasted", poured out on the ground in memory of that ever-faithful supply in the desert. But Jesus interrupts. He stands and beckons to the crowd, *"If anyone is thirsty, let him come to me and drink. Whoever believes in me, as the Scripture has said, streams of living water will flow from within them"* (John 7:37-38). Where Moses gave them water from a rock, Jesus declared that he is that rock (see also 1 Corinthians 10:4). He is the source of the living water. He doesn't just give living water; he is the Living Water.

All of that means that the Story of God's plan continues through Jesus. It is in him that we have life (John 1:4) and we are invited to drink. It is in him that we become the children of God (John 1:12). It is in him that we are invited to become part of the story. He is the fulfillment of the Old Testament, and the one to whom the story points. And it is in him that the story continues. The focus of God's plan now is Jesus. He is the New Beginning. We are now invited to begin with him.

7

INTO THE FIRE, PART 2

Acts 2:1-18

I N THE LAST CHAPTER we were discussing Jesus, baptism and "living water springing up to eternal life." We mentioned Moses leading Israel through the Red Sea, from death to life. We also compared water from the rock in the wilderness (Exodus 17:1-7) with Jesus' call for the thirsty to come to him (John 7:37, see also 1 Corinthians 10:4). We remembered Joshua leading Israel through the Jordan River into the Land of Promise. We talked about Jesus' baptism– and baptizing (John 3:22)–and what it meant. We also should parallel the forty days of spying out the Land, the forty years of wilderness wandering, and Jesus' own forty days in the desert of fasting and testing. But what is absolutely essential to the story is another passage, another baptism.

Jesus was crucified, his death certified (Mark 15:44-45), and his body placed in a tomb. The tomb was sealed and guarded. One thing that all four of the gospels recount, with differing detail, is that on the third day, on the day after the Sabbath, came a new First Day, a New Beginning. The gospels agree, "on the First Day of the week, while it was still dark", as the women went grieving to Jesus' grave, they were shocked to meet angels instead, who informed the women that Jesus was, indeed, most certainly not dead, that he was alive. Then, for forty days (do you notice a pattern?), Jesus appeared to them, to many witnesses (1 Corinthians 15:3-8), walked with them, ate with them (Luke 24:41-43), taught them and showed himself to them (Acts 1:3).

Paul said this about that: *We were buried with him in baptism...* (Romans 6:4). The "sign of Jonah" (Matthew 12:38-40)–the deliverance after three days in the belly of a great fish (Jonah 1:17)–the resurrection on the third day–is compared to passing, once again, through the water. We are buried with him. Our baptism is emblematic of the death of Jesus, the days in the grave, and the resurrection. So that we die with him and are raised to new life. In Jesus, we become new creatures (2 Corinthians 5:17). The old life is done and new life's begun. We have passed with him through the waters. We now drink of him: the living water that gives life.

We can now move on.

In chapter 3, we looked at the place that fire has in the story – the burning bush where God called Moses (Exodus 3:1ff); the pillar of fire that guarded Israel in the desert (Exodus 13:21); the continual fire on the altar (Leviticus 6:8-13); fire from heaven in answer to David's prayer of repentance (1 Chronicles 21:26), in response to Elijah's prayer (1 Kings 18:16-42), and at Solomon's dedication of the temple (2 Chronicles 7:1); fire that consumed Gideon's offering (Judges 6:20-22); and the three young men who walked unscathed in Nebuchadnezzar's fiery furnace (Daniel 3). Those are just a few of the places where fire appears to play a role in the story of God's Grand Plan.

The image of God as fire was deeply imprinted on the minds of Israel. In Exodus 24, as Moses is on the mountain with God, we read, *To the Israelites the glory of the LORD looked like a consuming fire on top of the mountain* (Exodus 24:17). Moses used that image to reinforce the idea that God alone is to be worshiped: *"For the LORD your God is a consuming fire, a jealous God"* (Deuteronomy 4:24). David's song of praise, repeated in 2 Samuel 22 and Psalm 18, in reflecting on God's deliverance from his enemies, says, *"Smoke rose from his nostrils; consuming fire came from his mouth, burning coals came out of it"* (2 Samuel 22:9; Psalm 18:8). Noting that God is both a God of compassion and grace, and a God of justice, who *binds up the bruises of his people and heals the wounds he has inflicted*, Isaiah waxes poetic: *See the Name of the LORD comes from afar, with burning anger and dense clouds of smoke; his lips are full of wrath, and his tongue is a consuming fire* [as he] *shakes the nations in the sieve of destruction* (Isaiah 30:26-28). Regarding the godless, Isaiah asks, *"Who of us can dwell with the consuming fire?"* (Isaiah 33:14).

So in the New Testament, the writer of Hebrews (Hebrews 12), in reminding the Church that God demands *holiness* (v. 14) and *disciplines us for our good* (v. 10), reminds us that through Christ, we have come with *a great cloud of witnesses* (v. 1),... *to a mountain that cannot be touched and that is burning with fire* (v. 18),... *to the city of the living God, the heavenly Jerusalem.... in joyful assembly* (v. 22),... *to Jesus the mediator of a new covenant* (v. 24)... *Therefore, since we are receiving a kingdom that cannot be shaken, let us be thankful, and so worship God acceptably with reverence and awe, for our "God is a consuming fire"* (vv. 28-29).

Why is all of this important to the story? It is because of the nature of fire itself. But it is also because of the nature of God. The Glorious Presence of God, the *shekinah*, is indicated in the Bible, through those Old Testament references, with fire. Let's be clear though: fire was not a god; fire itself was not to be worshiped. But God's Glorious Presence seems to have come with fire – on the mountain, on the altar, in the tabernacle and then the temple. God often appeared as fire. If God is like fire, we must understand something about fire.

Fire protects. Ask anyone who has spent the night "where the wild things are"[11]. A good camp fire keeps the wild animals away. To the wilderness wanderers, it was a pillar of fire at night that let them know they were safe, that God was watching over and protecting them.

Fire comforts. I remember a trip my wife and I took to the Oregon coast. It was a cold, stormy January. I went outside to watch the waves and feel the strength of the wind. But when I went back

---

[11] Maurice Sendak, *Where the Wild Things Are* (New York: HarperCollins, 1963)

inside, the fire in the fireplace warmed and comforted me. When "the weather outside is frightful, the fire is so delightful."[12]

Fire destroys. Many have seen the damage done to a home when a fire has swept through it. Not only are the walls and roof charred, and not only are the things we possess gone, but more ephemeral things are gone as well – photographs, heirlooms, wedding and baby albums, and the marks on the door-frame that show how our children have grown. Uncontrolled fire costs us dearly.

Fire consumes. What we've built turns to ashes and smoke. Things burned are not just damaged, they are often completely consumed by the fire. We've seen news stories of homes that seem to have vanished after a wild fire has burned through a community. A few years ago, we watched as a fire burned whole neighborhoods in the vicinity of Colorado Springs, Colorado. Where neighbors lived and children played – just gone, vanished. Only smoke and ash remained.

But fire also purifies. In speaking of the coming Messiah, Malachi invokes the image of a metal-smith melting ore to produce fine silver – *Who can stand when he appears? For he will be like a refiner's fire... He will sit as a refiner and purifier of silver; he will purify the Levites and refine them like gold and silver. Then the LORD will have men who will bring offerings of righteousness...* (Malachi 3:3). Jeremiah also – *Therefore this is what the LORD Almighty says: "See I will refine and test them, for what else can I do because of the sin of my people?"* (Jeremiah 9:7).

---

[12] "Let It Snow", lyrics by Sammy Cahn

Regarding the righteous remnant of Zechariah's prophecy, God says, *"This third I will bring into the fire; I will refine them like silver and test them like gold"* (Zechariah 13:9). These images speak to cleansing from sin, purifying a holy people for God. Remember what we've been saying about the intended uniqueness of Israel – they were to be a *"kingdom of priests and a holy nation"* (Exodus 19:6). And throughout Exodus, Numbers, Leviticus, and Deuteronomy, they were constantly being called to cleanse themselves – not just physically by bathing, but to remove idols and sin from their lives. Recently there was published a video clip in which the wife of a prominent television preacher proclaimed that God's plan for us is our happiness. In response, we need to emphasize this: Jesus did not come to make us happy; he came to make us holy. God desires a holy people, cleansed from sin, purified and refined as gold and silver. *Jesus suffered outside the city gate,* the writer to the Hebrews said, *to make the people holy* (Hebrews 13:12).

Thus the Psalmist prayed, *"Create in me a pure heart, O God"* (Psalm 51:10). I grew up hearing this: *"Who may ascend the hill of the LORD? Who may stand in his holy place? He who has clean hands and a pure heart, who does not lift up his soul to an idol or swear by what is false"* (Psalm 24:3-4). "Clean hands", of course, means not guilty of violence or oppression. But a purified heart is required of one who would stand in the holy place.

In response to Isaiah's confession of sinfulness in the vision of God's throne room, an angel, identified as a seraph (a burning one), took a live coal from the altar and touched it to Isaiah's lips.

And he laid it upon my mouth, and said: Lo, this hath touched thy lips; and thine iniquity is taken away, and thy sin purged (Isaiah 6:7, KJV).

So John the Baptist described the Messiah as one who *will baptize you with the Holy Spirit and with fire* (Matthew 3:11), and who burns *up the chaff with unquenchable fire* (Matthew 3:12). If God's Glorious Presence is symbolized by fire, then when *the Word became flesh* (John 1:14), we should expect that *we have seen his glory* (John 1:14) should include something of fire. And it does: Jesus birth was accompanied by a star, the star that guided the Magi to the Holy Family was a sign of fire.

Jesus also used fiery images frequently. He referred often to a place of burning, Gehenna, which gives us our image of hell, as a place of final punishment, a place of eternal destruction. Those fires destroy and do not comfort. But another fire was to come as a purifying force and a sign of God's presence.

Most Christians are familiar with the story of that first Pentecost in Acts 2. Gentile Christians, which most of us are, may not be as familiar with all the ramifications of this day.

For the Jew, Pentecost is the festival of Shavuot, or the Feast of Weeks.[13] It comes seven weeks[14]

---

[13] Ben M. Edidin, *Jewish Customs and Ceremonies* (New York: Hebrew Publishing Company, 1941), p. 164

[14] Forty days plus one week. The parallel is the time that Noah spent on the ark after it came to rest "on the mountains of Ararat". After forty days, Noah sent out a raven and a dove. The dove returned. After another seven days, Noah sent the dove again, which returned with an olive branch,

after Passover, and pilgrims would bring the first pickings of grapes, figs, pomegranates, and more to offer as a thank offering. It is also known, then, as the Feast of First Fruits. It is given another name, significantly, The Giving of the Law, for it commemorates the day that Moses brought the Ten Commandments down from Mt. Sinai. It is a day of singular identity for the Jews, highly significant for the giving of the Torah, the Law that sets them apart as *a kingdom of priests and a holy nation* (Exodus 19:6). Shavuot (Pentecost) is especially important for Jews who do not live in Israel, for it connects them with their history and identifies them as a people, as Jews, and as descendants of Abraham. It is important for us to remember that the first disciples of Jesus were all Jews who would have eagerly celebrated the great feasts of their people.

So, as Jews celebrating a signal moment in their history, *when the day of Pentecost came the disciples were all together in one place. Suddenly a sound like the blowing of a violent wind came from heaven and filled the whole house where they were sitting. They saw what seemed to be tongues of fire that separated and came to rest on each of them. All of them were filled with the Holy Spirit...* (Acts 2:1-4).

---

the first fruits of the post-flood world. Genesis 8:4-11. It was yet another week before Noah and his family left the safety of the ark, after the dove, sent out a third time, did not return. There appears to be a further parallel of Noah's "freedom" from the confinement of the ark, and Passover as Israel's freedom from Egyptian slavery. This pattern of rescue to a restored/recreated world is repeated throughout the Bible.

Just as the Glorious Presence of God was evidenced by the pillar of fire resting over the tabernacle and filling the newly-dedicated temple, so the fire of God rested on that first Pentecost gathering of the Church. Some will debate whether the signs of Pentecost were inaugural signs or normative for the Church. We have no need to engage that debate, but only to point out that the Glorious Presence was on the Church that day in the same way that the Glorious Presence rested on the tabernacle in the wilderness and then on Solomon's temple.

Flames of fire indicate two things to us: First, the very presence of God, the filling of the Holy Spirit; and second, the refining fire of the Messiah, the purification of a holy nation. As the mountain appeared to be covered in fire, so this people of the Messiah appeared to be covered with fire. As the three Hebrews walked in the fires of Nebuchadnezzar's furnace, so the 120 in the upper room walked in the fire of God's presence. They were baptized with fire as John the Baptists had prophesied.

John's gospel connects Pentecost with Shavuot with these words: *For the law was given through Moses; grace and truth came through Jesus Christ* (John 1:17). The giving of the Law on the one hand, and the giving of the Spirit on the other. The apostle Paul spent a lot of space in the letter to the Romans distinguishing the Law from Grace – two laws, as he describes them, *the law of the Spirit of life set me free from the law of sin and death* (Romans 8:2).

The New Testament writers continually call us to move toward that fire, to move into that purifying, refining fire. We are to *make every effort... to be holy;* [for] *without holiness no one will see the Lord* (Hebrews 12:14). *It is God's will that you should be sanctified* (1 Thessalonians 4:3), that is, that you should be made holy. Jesus commanded, *"Be perfect, therefore, as your heavenly Father is perfect"* (Matthew 5:48). Paul addresses the church at Corinth, that divided, chaotic, and argumentative church, as *those sanctified in Christ Jesus and called to be holy* (1 Corinthians1:2).

Peter, recalling Moses' instruction in Leviticus (11:44-45; 19:1; 20:7), calls on the Church to *be holy in all you do; for it is written: "Be holy, because I am holy"* (1 Peter 1:15-16). After describing the kind of life that will lead to, Peter reminds us that God still desires a holy people to complete his Grand Plan. He still wants a kingdom of priests. Peter believed that, through Christ, through Messiah Jesus, the Church is the new Israel; the Church steps in where Israel has failed. Noting that Israel has rejected the "precious stone", Peter wrote, *As you come to him, the living stone – rejected by men but chosen by God and precious to him – you also, like living stones, are being built into a spiritual house to be a holy priesthood, offering spiritual sacrifices to God through Jesus Christ.... But you are a chosen people, a royal priesthood, a holy nation, a people belonging to God, that you may declare the praises of him who called you out of darkness into his wonderful light* (1 Peter 2:4-9). The Church was a new nation, a new people, the people of God, forged in the fires of Pentecost and baptized with the Holy Spirit and with fire.

God began with humans created in the "image and likeness of God". But those first humans disobeyed and defaced God's good creation. He called Israel to be "a kingdom of priests and a holy nation" to fulfill his plan of restoration and reconciliation. As we've discovered, they failed because they wanted to be like everyone else. So, through Jesus, God calls us to be holy, so that through us he may complete his grand plan and reconcile the world to himself and restore his good creation.

8

HEAVEN'S
JUST A WAYSIDE

Revelation 21:1-5; Revelation 22:1-5
Romans 8:18-25; 1 Corinthians 15:35-57

I N CHAPTER FIVE I wrote that some
people think the Old and New Testaments
are like parallel roads that never meet. There
are those who believe the Old Testament tells one
story – for the Jews; and the New Testament tells
a different story – for Christians. Some refer to the
parts as the "Jewish Scriptures" and the "Christian
Scriptures". I've heard Christians say that the Old
Testament is not important, that we don't really
need it at all, that Jesus did away with the Old on
the cross. They will quote (out of context) a verse
or two from Romans or Corinthians or another of
Paul's letters as some sort of proof.

However, they are wrong. As we have discovered, and as we will continue to discover, the Old
Testament presents the first half of the story, and is
quite incomplete without the New — and the New
Testament presents the second half of the story and

does not quite make sense without the Old. With either, you are getting only half of the story. The New Testament writers were quite dependent on the Old Testament. They quoted from it often and referred to it much more often. In fact, every reference to "scripture" in the New Testament is a reference to the Old Testament. Sometimes the writers would overtly quote a passage from Deuteronomy, the Psalms, or the Prophets, and sometimes even say, "The prophets said..." But more often it is a subtle reference, with a knowing wink and a smile, as if to say, "You know what I'm talking about."

Well, those first readers certainly would have known, but we are not as familiar with the Old Testament as we should be. That means that those "nudge, nudge, wink, wink" references are often lost on us. For example, we read the story of the Passover in Exodus and usually only notice that the Last Supper took place on Passover – missing the fact that the Last Supper of Jesus was actually a celebration and fulfillment of the Passover. We miss the parallels between Moses and Jesus, between the Red Sea and Jesus' own baptism, or, as I pointed out last chapter, the amazing parallels of the forty days.

Now, just as the New Testament writers did with their audience, I have to assume that you know the story up to this point. But let's take just a quick moment to review one or two things – God, extravagant in creation, filled the earth with beauty and life. Genesis 1 is a temple narrative[15] with

---

[15] John H. Walton, *The Lost World of Genesis One* (Downers Grove: InterVarsity Press, 2009)

God making a place for himself and an "image" of himself to inhabit the temple. He declared it all "very good" (Genesis 1:31) Then sin entered the picture, and death with sin. The man and the woman ate fruit from the Tree of the Knowledge of Good and Evil. By the way, it was *not* simply the Tree of Knowledge – that's a serious misunderstanding. They knew good because they knew God. The only thing this tree could give them was the knowledge of evil. God exiled them from the Garden and sealed off the way to the Tree of Life. I asked you then to remember this tree, the Tree of Life, for it would show up again.

You understand that the rest of the story is a story of exile and deliverance. Slaves in Egypt were delivered through the Red Sea. Wanderers, exiles, in the desert were delivered into the Land of Promise through the Jordan River. Exiled to Babylon, they returned at the order of Cyrus and under the leadership of Ezra and Nehemiah. They were never satisfied with Moses, never satisfied with the Judges, never satisfied to be the *kingdom of priests* and *holy nation* that God desired them to be, never satisfied to be uniquely the people of God. They wanted to be just like everyone else with kings. Even the kings did not satisfy them. But God is a God of New Beginnings. He promised another prophet like Moses (Deuteronomy 18:15, 18), and another king for David's throne (Isaiah 9:7). He promised a Savior, a Servant, a Shepherd (Isaiah 40:11; Ezekiel 34), a virgin's son (Isaiah 7:14) who would come in like a king on a donkey (Zechariah 9:9), suffer like a criminal, and then see the light of life (Isaiah 53:1-12).

The central feature in the story is the one that points most decisively toward the resolution. It is the resurrection of Jesus. That is where we turn now.

Everyone dies. That is a given. We describe ourselves as "mortal". Our word is from the Latin word *mortis*, meaning "death". That is, we describe ourselves as dying, always dying, as compared to God, immortal, never dying. It is a fact of life, which everyone accepts even as we do all we can to delay and deny it. Death is so ingrained in our psyche that we see no way around it. We try medicine and magic to overcome it. Modern science allures us with the idea of cryogenics, that perhaps we might freeze our bodies just prior to death, or at the moment of death, to give medical science time to find a cure, revive us, and give us another shot at immortality. So, to say that Jesus died, is almost nonsensical – of course, he did. Because everybody dies.

But Jesus defeated death. He rose, bodily, alive, breathing, eating, talking to the disciples. They saw him. At first they didn't believe it. The gospel writers tell us that they thought they were seeing a ghost, but the facts were undeniable. There he was. Paul tells us that Jesus was also seen alive by over 500 at once time, some of whom were still living and able to serve as corroborating witnesses in AD 57 when Paul wrote those words (1 Corinthians 15:6). The risen-from-the-dead Jesus was also seen by other individuals and groups over a period of forty days. They watched as Jesus left, rising into the air to be obscured by a cloud (Acts 1:9-11). The resurrection of Jesus became the central tenet of the Christian faith. It is the singular event that validates everything else.

If Jesus had only died we would never have heard of him – or of the disciples. His death may have been sacrificial, may have been for our salvation, may have reconciled us to God – but we would have never known it without the resurrection. Paul makes the case in 1 Corinthians 15 that the resurrection is essential to every other aspect of the Christian faith.

But – and here's the kicker – Jesus was just the first. The *first fruits of those who have fallen asleep*, is the way he says it. Jesus defeated sin on the cross. When he emerged from the tomb, he had defeated death. His promise, one of the "I AM" declarations, was *"I AM the resurrection and the life..."* (John 11:25). Even there, Jesus promised that *whoever lives and believes in* [him] *will never die* (John 11:26). The Greek actually says, *"...will not die forever"* [οὐ μὴ ἀποθάνῃ εισ τιν αιωνα]. *"Will never die"* has been taken to mean that death is no longer in our future, that we will live forever. The problem with that is that we still die. But Jesus said that we *will not die forever*. That means that though death remains part of our earthly existence, it has lost it's power. Death is no longer the end and there is hope beyond the grave, beyond death, beyond "heaven" as we have usually defined it.

Now, before we continue, we have a problem with our definition (and description) of heaven. I do not know where it came from, but we have gotten the idea that we go to heaven or hell when we die (or, if you're Catholic, perhaps to purgatory). In thirty-plus years of doing funerals, I have yet to meet any family that did not think their loved one went to heaven, where "they're looking down on us". Apparently, nobody is bad enough to go to hell.

Our conception of heaven is a place of light, color, music, joy, floating on clouds, getting wings and a halo, and (I hate to say it) a bunch of other boring stuff, which we do forever and ever, world without end. Our concept of "eternity" is *a very long time*. But in the Bible eternity has nothing to do with the passing of days, months, or years. *Eternal* appears to be a quality of life rather than a quantity. That is, as we discovered earlier, eternal life is *life from above*.

The Bible doesn't teach much about heaven – at least not the way we've conceived of it. Paul wrote about preferring to be absent from the body to be with the Lord (2 Corinthians 5:8). The word, "heaven", is used, but there is no Biblical support for our common conception of heaven. Jesus said he was going to prepare a place (John 14:1-4), and Paul talks about our heavenly dwelling (2 Corinthians 5). But in the context of the whole of Scripture, it most certainly does not mean what we thought it meant.

Romans 8 speaks of the liberation of creation from bondage and groaning (v. 21), of a redemption of our bodies (v. 23), of an eager expectation (v. 19) for some future glory (v. 18).

The entire story, the meta-narrative of the Bible is one of exile and restoration – from the exile from the garden, the flood, the time of the judges, the Babylonian exile. The Old Testament tells the story of the exile, the estrangement of man from God.

Jews continue to long for the end of the exile. For them it is not over. They are still scattered, dispersed (hence the Diaspora) across the earth. But the New Testament tells how God intends to end the exile and restore Creation to it's original beauty and intent.

Jesus frequently used marriage language and parables to illustrate God's reconciling plan. For example, in John 14, when Jesus told the disciples that he was going away to prepare a place for them, he was using a marriage image. When the betrothal is made, the groom-to-be, would go home to the family *insula* (compound). There, under the supervision of his father, the young man would build the apartment that would be his bride's home. When the home was complete to the father's satisfaction, the young man would return to collect his bride, the wedding would take place, and the new couple would move into their new home. *"In my Father's house are many rooms"* (John 14:2).

Romans 8 declares that creation groans for release. 1 Corinthians 15 tells of the centrality of the resurrection, first of Jesus, and then of the followers of Christ, in the work of reconciliation. There Paul talks about the resurrection body. His illustration is of the different sorts of "flesh" – birds, fish, animals, and man. But he takes "flesh" – or matter – even further: there is a different sort of matter (or splendor) about the earth, about the sun, about the stars. The varieties of "splendor", or matter, or flesh, serves to illustrate the difference between what is mortal and what is spiritual.

Now please note this carefully: Paul does *not* use "spiritual" as the opposite of "physical", but as the opposite of "natural". Both spiritual and natural are physical; that is, both are real, substantial, and material. But what is natural is of earth; what is spiritual is of God. And the resurrection of Jesus is the illustration Paul uses. Jesus died physically and rose physically. But he died naturally and rose spiritually – not as a spirit, but as a real, material, physical person. The resurrection transformed his body. It changed from mortal (dying) to immortal (undying), all the while remaining physical. It is vital that we understand the intent of Paul's words in 1 Corinthians 15:35-57, when he talks about the resurrection body. Not material vs. immaterial; physical vs. spiritual; but natural material vs. spiritual material. Not ghostly, but solid.[16] But the very nature of the physical is now changed. *We will not all sleep* (die), *but we will all be changed... the perishable* (natural) *must clothe itself with the imperishable* (spiritual) (1 Corinthians 15:51-54).

That happens when the resurrection takes place – not Jesus' resurrection, but ours. The Bible is not clear at all about what happens between death and the resurrection. There is, apparently, a place of rest, where we are "with Christ", a wayside, if you will, that we call "heaven." But heaven is just a wayside – it is not the goal. Nor is it the end. We do not end in death – as Jesus said, *"He who lives and believes in me will not die forever"* (John 11:26).

So, here's what we find: It is part of John's vision in Revelation 21 and 22. There is a new

---

[16] See C.S. Lewis' description of heaven in The Great Divorce, beginning with chapter 3.

heaven and a new earth – the old has "passed away". Jesus used a lot of marriage illustrations in his parables – *I am going to prepare a place for you* (John 14:2) is a marriage metaphor. Now the "new Jerusalem" is prepared as a bride – reminiscent of Paul's words in Ephesians 5:21-33, where he writes about husbands and wives and submission, but, he says, *"I am talking about Christ and the church."* And *the dwelling of God is with men, and he will live with them* (Revelation 21:3) as husband and wife live together.

But I want you to see what it looks like. Revelation 22. *Then the angel showed me the river of the water of life* (v. 1). Where did we see the promise of "living water"? (John 4:1, 13-14; 7:36-37). But it was also *a river watering the garden* in Genesis 2:10. *On each side of the river stood the tree of life* (v. 2). Where have we seen the tree of life? It was the one from which God exiled Adam and Eve and sealed in the Garden (Genesis 3:22). It was the tree upon which Jesus died, for *the life is in the blood* (Leviticus 17:11-14), and *without the shedding of blood there is no forgiveness* (Hebrews 9:22). The tree of life reappears here with *leaves for the healing of the nations* (v. 2).

And there is no more curse (v. 3). What was the curse? *The wages of sin is death* (Romans 6:23). The curse in the garden was that eating the forbidden fruit brought death, and pain, and hard labor, and reluctant crops beset with weeds (Genesis 3:14-19). *He will wipe every tear from their eyes. There will be no more death or mourning or crying or pain, for the old order of things has passed away* (Revelation 21:4). Take the time to read both of these final chapters.

Read them slowly and savor the words and the pictures they present. Dream of the beauty John is trying to describe. You will come at last to this –

I did not see a temple in the city, because the Lord God Almighty and the Lamb are its temple. The city does not need the sun or the moon to shine on it, for the glory of God gives it light, and the Lamb is its lamp. The nations will walk by its light... Nothing impure will ever enter it, nor will anyone who does what is shameful or deceitful... (Revelation 22:22-27). Remember that I told you that Genesis 1 is a temple narrative? God built a temple and set his image in it. The image, and the temple along with it, was defiled. But here the temple is rebuilt and the image restored – *and the dwelling of God is with man... and God himself will be with them...* (Revelation 21:3).

Here is also the symbolism of the pillar of cloud/fire in the wilderness, the Glorious Presence in Solomon's temple, and the "tongues of fire" at Pentecost find fulfillment. No longer is there a need for a "sign" of God's Glorious Presence, for the *Shekinah* will have become reality to us in a new way. We will experience it face-to-face.

John saw the city. Oh, yes, he did. But Paul anticipated the City when he wrote, *I consider that our present sufferings are not worth comparing with the glory that will be revealed in us. The creation waits in eager expectation for the sons of God to be revealed. For the creation was subjected to frustration, not by its own choice, but by the will of the one who subjected it, in hope that the creation itself will be liberated from its bondage to decay and brought into the glorious freedom of the children of God. We know that the whole creation has been groaning as in the pains of childbirth right up to the present time. Not only so, but we ourselves, who have the firstfruits of the Spirit, groan inwardly was we wait eagerly for our adoption as sons, the redemption of our bodies. For in this hope we were saved...* (Romans 8:18-24).

That is the story. That is our destiny. That is the rest that remains for the people of God (Hebrews 4:9). That is why Israel was supposed to be, and why the Church is supposed to be *a kingdom of priests and a holy nation* (Exodus 19:6; 1 Peter 2:9). We are an outpost of the Kingdom, and the heralds of the Resurrection, called to be holy (1 Corinthians 1:2) and to live lives worthy of Christ (Romans 16:2; Ephesians 4:1; Philippians 1:27; Colossians 1:10; 1 Thessalonians 2:12).

Part 2

BIG PICTURE ISSUES

READING THE BIBLE AS a single story has implications for other things that Christians have come to believe. Because we have tended to read the Bible as a collection of stories and to preach and memorize bits and pieces apart from their larger context, we also have tended to take each of the following issues in isolation from the rest of the Bible story. There are, of course, translation issues that arise because of the dynamic nature of the English language. But the major problem has always been that we have not viewed the various issues within the context of the whole.

When questions arise, as they often do, we tend to look within the selected text for interpretation. May I suggest that it would be valuable to look outside the questioned text for clues? John Wesley referred often to the "general tenor" of the Scripture. He also believed that the best way to interpret Scripture is with other Scripture. That is, let the Bible tell it's whole story and let it interpret itself. We find the meaning of any verse, chapter, or story grows richer and fuller when the whole of the Bible is allowed to speak. What follows are some selected issues raised, and perhaps answered, when we read the Bible as one story.

9

A LITTLE SOMETHING ABOUT CHRISTMAS

THE CHRISTMAS SEASON presents a bit of a conundrum for some Christians. On the one hand, it is supposed to be a celebration of Christ. On the other it has become a season of sales and pressure to purchase gifts for no other reason than that it is "customary". There is an unspoken demand to spend, spend, and spend some more. From "black Friday" to "small business Saturday" and "cyber Monday" to the countdown sales: "Just twelve more days until Christmas!" The on-line businesses touting "next day delivery" got shipping companies in a bind because they were swamped with orders and could not deliver what the merchants had promised.

People camp out for days to be first in line when the sale opens for some new gizmo and then stampede when the doors open. Then come the fights over limited stock, the theft, the commercial gimmicks: including "lay-away", credit cards, and time-limited specials – all designed to separate the customer from her money. Cheap decorations fill the aisles. And then the "drive-through" neighbor-hoods where families compete to create the most elaborate light display around their homes. Not only is the competition fierce, within and between neighborhoods, but society rewards that competition with evening news coverage. There was even a television show[17] pitting residents in competition for the best-decorated home, awarding a prize for what appears to me to be the most outrageous-ly-decorated, most brightly-lit home in the nation. These "Christmas decoration wars", encourage gaudy, cluttered, and expensive "light shows" that consume massive amounts of electricity in pursuit of the prize.

The unspoken assumption is that "Christmas" is about shopping, decorating, gifts, parties, and spending. Buy, buy, buy. Spend, spend, spend. And most of what is offered, if we were honest about it, is overpriced, unneeded–and mostly unwanted–junk.

And because Christmas is about shopping, Christ is mostly excluded. In some cases, Jesus is just neglected, ignored in the commercial rush. In some cases, Jesus is exploited, used as a gim-mick to sell religiously-oriented "junk". In some cases, Jesus is the object of hostility and deliberate exclusion. We seem to want a Christmas without Christ, as seen in a grade-school version of "Silent Night" that made no mention of "round yon virgin Mother and Child, holy Infant so tender and mild." There was an atheist comment proclaiming that

---

[17] The Great Christmas Light Fight, ABC network – http://abc.go.com/shows/the-great-christmas-light-fight

Christ is not necessary for Christmas. There is also a plethora of "holidays" deliberately dropped into the season: Kwanzaa, an African-American invention[18] of recent decades invested with mostly secular and pagan ideology; Festivus, an invention of the Jerry Seinfeld television show, "the holiday for the rest of us". Some attempt to return to ancient pagan roots by celebrating the winter solstice, the Norse Yule, or the Roman Saturnalia.

In the "run-up" to Christmas in 2013, a federal judge ordered the removal of the Mt. Soledad war memorial cross in San Diego, California, condemning it (again) as a violation of the "separation of church and state". The usual suspects continue to be engaged in forcing removal of manger scenes–often substituting them for other religious symbols, such as a Hanukkah menorah, Satanic symbols or atheist signs. And the usual debates over whether to include religious music in school concerts, although the only "problem" seems to be with music of a Christian nature.

Then there is the line-up of holiday entertainment and sappy television specials, most of them with a "what it's all about" tagline of some sort–family, giving, togetherness, or love. "It's a Wonderful Life", as good and meaningful as it is, gets old when it is shown year after year. Hollywood has a line-up of cartoons about Frosty, Rudolph, misfit toys, and Santa Claus, "the elf on the shelf" and the "Christmas fairy". Some folks are in the habit of seeing "Living Christmas Trees"

---

[18] Maulana Karenga created Kwanzaa in 1966. See https:// en.wikipedia.org/wiki/Kwanzaa

or the wonderful ballet, *The Nutcracker*. The ballet is beautiful and "Miracle on 34th Street" tugs at the heart. But, really, what does any of that have to do with Christmas?

The same thing could be asked of churches which try to get in on the entertainment... excuse me, *ministry*... aspect of the season. We put on living Christmas tree concerts, living Nativities, cantatas, and children's programs, all with the goal of getting people in the door. Grandparents snap cute photos, and drive-by spectators sigh at the beauty or tenderness of the Nativity (and wonder where you got a camel). But we get the same results as those who decorate their neighborhoods – we drive through admiringly, but we don't live there! Perhaps that is the problem – we invite people to come visit, but we don't expect them to live here. In some ways, perhaps, we encourage the "C&E" church attendance pattern (Christmas and Easter). One has to wonder, in regard to most of what we do at Christmas: what does it really have to do with Christmas? Or Christ?

Christmas was not celebrated for much of Church history. In the first centuries of the church, because the date of Christ's birth was unknown, it was not added to the calendar. The first creche, or manger scene, is thought to be one built by St. Francis of Assisi in the 13th Century, using live animals. The first Christmas tree is thought to be one brought indoors and decorated with candles by Martin Luther in the 16th Century (candles turned out to be a particularly bad idea). Puritan English refused to celebrate Christmas, considering it either pagan or "Romish"–a reference to the

Roman Catholic Church–and rejected because it was Catholic: Christ's Mass. It is true that many of our holiday traditions have some pagan origin but have been appropriated and given new meaning by the Church. In our day, there are those who refuse to celebrate Christmas for these two reasons: we don't know Jesus actual date of birth; and Christmas is largely (in their view) a pagan holiday. It is true that the Church appropriated the Roman Saturnalia and made it a Christian holiday, Christmas, by superimposing the supposed date of Jesus' birth over it.

It is also interesting that the earliest Christian creed, found in 1 Corinthians 15:3-5, contains no mention of Jesus' birth: *For what I received I passed on to you as of first importance: that Christ **died** for our sins according to the Scriptures, that he was **buried**, that he was **raised** on the third day according to the Scriptures, and that he **appeared**...* A measure of how important the birth was to the Early Church is the fact that only two of the gospel accounts, Matthew and Luke, include nativity narratives, and the Gospel of Mark, considered to be the oldest, does not. The two nativity narratives are included for specific reasons, and beyond these two narratives there is no further mention of Jesus' birth in the New Testament.

So why did Matthew and Luke include a birth narrative?

Matthew–the importance of prophecy

First, it is possible that the influence of Matthew shows up in the early creed Paul quotes in 1 Corinthians 15. Paul notes two items that are "according to Scripture." Matthew's meta-narrative in the gospel is that Jesus fulfilled prophecy; that is, Jesus is the Messiah because he is the fulfillment of the Scriptures. It is Matthew who quotes Jesus as saying, *"Do not think that I have come to abolish the Law or the Prophets: I have not come to abolish them but to fulfill them"* (Matthew 5:17).

For the Jew, the Messiah would have to meet certain criteria set down by the prophets in ages past. It is thus important, from the outset, for Matthew to demonstrate that Jesus did just that. The birth narrative is vital for Matthew to establish Jesus as the Messiah.

He begins with what is often described as too boring and repetitious to be of interest. I often hear Christians wondering about the "begats" in Matthew 1. They often just skip over this section and consider it irrelevant. However, the "begats" play a vital role for Matthew. When we understand Matthew's purpose, they will take on new vitality for us as well.

The Messiah was supposed to be a descendant of King David. There was to be a man on David's throne forever. Isaiah 11:1-3, considered a Messianic prophecy, predicts *a shoot...from the stump of Jesse... The Spirit of the LORD will rest on him – the Spirit of wisdom and of understanding, the Spirit of counsel and of power, the Spirit of knowledge...* King David was the son of Jesse. Jeremiah 23:5-6 prophesies a day when God will *raise up to David a righteous Branch, a King who will reign wisely... In his days, Judah will be saved...* The Messiah was to be a savior for Israel. Then Ezekiel 34:23-24 foretells *one shepherd, my servant David, and he will tend them... my servant David will be prince among them.* So Matthew begins by identifying Jesus as *the son of David, the son of Abraham* (Matthew 1:1). The genealogy, then, is designed to prove Jesus' lineage as the descendant of David, and that Jesus is, rightfully, the "son of David" "according to the Scripture."

We continue to see Matthew's reference to prophecy throughout the birth narrative. Jesus was born of a virgin (Matthew 1:18) in keeping with Isaiah 7:14 – *"The virgin will be with child and will give birth to a son, and will call him Immanuel."* He is given the name Jesus (Matthew 1:21), fulfilling Jeremiah 23:6 – *"In his days, Judah will be saved..."* The name Jesus is *Joshua,* or *Y'shua* in Hebrew (the Hebrew language has no "J"), referring us back to the great general Joshua, successor of Moses, who led Israel in possessing the Promised Land at the end of the Exodus. It is also linguistically connected to Hosea, the prophet who spoke of God's unfailing love for unfaithful Israel. Matthew makes the connection with Isaiah himself – *All this took place to fulfill what the Lord had said through the prophet...* and quoting that prophecy in 1:24 .

Matthew includes the story of the Magi because it, too, references the fulfillment of prophecy. Isaiah 49:7 predicts that *"Kings will see you and rise up, princes will see and bow down..."* Isaiah 60:3 says that *"Nations will come to your light, and kings to the brightness of your dawn."* Psalm 72, a royal psalm referring to a righteous king of Israel, promises that *The kings of Tarshish and of distant shores will bring tribute to him; the kings of Sheba and Seba will present him with gifts. All kings will bow down to him and all nations will serve him.* It is thus necessary for Matthew to demonstrate these prophecies ful-filled in Jesus.

The star the Magi followed is also a part of Matthew's purpose. He reaches back to Balaam's prophecies in Numbers 24 – *"I see him, but not now; I behold him, but not near. A star will come out of Jacob; a scepter will rise out of Israel"* (Numbers 24:17).

The Magi also serve as a vehicle for Matthew to demonstrate further fulfillment of prophecy in Jesus' birthplace: Matthew 2:3-6 echoes Micah 5:2. The escape to Egypt (2:13-15) reminds him of Hosea 11:1. Herod's maniacal slaughter of the innocents fulfills the dread prophecy of Jeremiah 31:15. Matthew even quotes extra-biblical sources as being fulfilled. When Joseph brings his family back from Egypt, they circumvent the domain of Herod Archelaus, and return to Nazareth (2:19-23), resulting in Jesus being *called a Nazarene* (not to be confused with "Nazirite"[19]), fulfilling a prophecy from an unknown source, but that does not appear in the Bible.[20]

The careful reader will follow along as Matthew continues the meta-narrative of the prophe-cy-fulfilling that surrounds Jesus and proves his

---

[19] See Numbers 6 and Judges 13

[20] One possibility is that Matthew was thinking of the Hebrew word *nezer* meaning Branch, see Isaiah 11:1. The difficulty with this suggestion is two-fold: only here does Matthew use the plural "prophets", perhaps indicating no specific reference; and Matthew was writing of Jesus' hometown, Nazareth. See John 1:46.

Messiahship. But we repeat the note that Matthew includes the birth narrative because it serves that meta-narrative. For Matthew, Jesus' birth helps to prove his identity as the Son of David, and thus that he is qualified to be the Messiah of the Jews.

Finally, Matthew did not include dates or names in many cases–the Magi are not named–because historicity is not his focus. Matthew does not focus on the "historical" Jesus, but on the Jesus who fulfilled prophecy.

Mark–the reason for omission

The gospel of Mark does not include a nativity narrative. Instead it begins with John the Baptist and *the beginning of the good news about Jesus the Messiah* (Mark 1:1). It would be speculation to try to give a definitive reason for Mark's omission of any birth narrative. However, Mark's audience was most likely Gentile believers in Rome. Roman mythology was similar in many ways to Greek mythology. The Ephesian goddess Artemis is the equivalent of the Roman Diana, for example. The overlap would suggest that Mark's gentile audience was familiar with the several gods and goddesses in the pantheon who were produced (or born) without the aid of one or the other parent. Artemis is supposed to have sprung from the head of Zeus and had no mother. In spite, Hera then produced Hephaestus without the aid of a father. Other Roman or Greek gods and goddesses also arose through "miraculous" births, among them Artemis, Perseus and Hecate. Perhaps Mark feared confusing his readers with a narrative that would include Jesus miraculous birth. Better, then, to skip to the beginning of Jesus' ministry.

Luke–the importance of eyewitness

Luke was apparently a Gentile convert. As such, we may assume that his reasons for including a birth narrative differ from Matthew's. We first meet Luke, historically, as a companion of Paul in the book of Acts. He appears to become a part of the story in Acts 16, where the writer of Acts uses the word "we" for the first time (16:10). Paul had traveled through the regions (provinces) of Phrygia and Galatia, then to Asia (the Roman province, not the continent) and the borders of Mysia and Bithynia, and from there to Troas (the ancient city-state of Troy). There, Paul saw the vision of the man of Macedonia calling. Until this point, the writer refers to "Paul and his companions" and "they". But now, *after Paul had seen the vision, we got ready...*, and Luke is now with them. We discover in Colossians 4:14 that he was a doctor, and he was with Paul near the end of the Apostle's life (2 Timothy 4:11). Luke may have been a native of Troas or the not-too-distance city of Ephesus, as evidenced by the time and location of that first "we" statement.

He was the author of two New Testament books written to one man, identified in both as Theophilus, "friend of God". Whether that is a name or a description of the recipient is unknown, but it is the link between the two letters. Acts begins, "In my former book, Theophilus, I wrote about all that Jesus began to do and to teach..."

Acts, then, is volume two of the set. The gospel is volume one. Both depend on Luke's purpose and method:

> *Many have undertaken to draw up an account of the things that have been fulfilled among us, just as they were handed down to us by those who from the first were **eyewitnesses** and servants of the word. Therefore, since I myself have carefully investigated everything from the beginning, it seemed good also to me to write an orderly account for you, most excellent Theophilus, so that you may know the certainty of the things you have been taught* (Luke 1:1-4).

One might get a first impression that Luke is also interested in the fulfillment of prophecy by that early phrase, "the things that have been fulfilled among us". There are places where Luke alludes to Jewish prophecy. Much of Mary's song reflects the song of Hannah (1 Samuel 2). He references Isaiah 40:3-5 in recording John's proclamation (3:4-6). And Isaiah 61:1-2 is the portion read by Jesus in the synagogue (4:18-19). Luke's focus, however, is not on prophecy but on the historicity of Jesus. The key is found in the word, "eyewitnesses." Luke is also concerned to write *an orderly account* so that Theophilus' knowledge of Jesus might be certain. That is, Jesus is a real person, who really lived and really did the things we've reported of him.

There are apparent similarities between the life of Jesus and the myths of some of the Greek and Roman gods. There would be understandable skepticism that perhaps the Jews had adapted mythology and applied it to their Messiah, that Christians may have elevated Jesus by use of the mythology. So, Theophilus may have begun to question what he had heard about Jesus. Luke's purpose, then, is to present the testimony of eyewitnesses to Jesus' life.

He takes care to name the eyewitnesses, where he can find names. For example, Luke names Simeon (2:24-32) and Anna (2:36-38). The shepherds are not named, not because they are unimportant, but likely because Luke did not discover their names. He gives historical information about them, material that is extraneous to mythology, such as Anna's status as a widow, the length of her marriage, and her current living conditions. Such information appears to have little if anything to do with the "story". But it helps to establish the historicity of the people and events.

In discussing the differences between the ancient myths, such as the Epic of Gilgamesh, and the Biblical account, historian Thomas Cahill notes that "there is in these tales a kind of specificity – a concreteness of detail, a concern to get things right – that convinces us that the writer has not doubt that each of the main events he chronicles *happened*."[21] Where mythology is concerned with the greatness of the heroes, history does not cover up human flaws. Histories include details

---

[21] Cahill, p. 127, emphasis his.

and specifics that point to the reality of the people and the events.

Luke pulls together extended accounts of certain individuals. The birth narrative of John the Baptist, with the service, vision, and song of Zechariah, even Mary's visit to her relative, Elizabeth, seem extraneous to the story of Jesus. They appear to be "stage dressing" around the birth narrative of Jesus. Luke's introduction assures Theophilus that he has spoken with people like Zechariah, Elizabeth, Mary, and others. This is not hear-say or rewritten myth.

Luke sets the account in a verifiable historical setting:

> *"In the time of Herod king of Judea..."* (1:5). Herod the Great was king from 37 BC to AD 4.

> *"In those days Caesar Augustus issued a decree...* (2:1). Augustus (Gaius Octavius) was *princeps* (emperor) from 31 BC to AD 14.[22] Imperial decrees were recorded.

> *"... Quirinius was governor of Syria."* (2:2). Whether or not the imperial records survive, or whether those records are today complete, this would also have been a matter of

---

[22] Michael Grant, *The Roman Emperors* (New York: Charles Scribner's Sons, 1985), pp 9-16

imperial record, easily verifiable to Theophilus.

Luke gives a time-line, of little value to myth, but vital to history. The time-line helps establish the credibility of the account.

Following Zechariah's vision, Elizabeth becomes pregnant. *In the sixth month* (1:26), God sent the angel to Mary. This could either be the sixth month of the year, or, as I believe, the sixth month of Elizabeth's pregnancy. I take this view because of Mary's subsequent visit to her relative, and the information given in 1:56 that *Mary stayed with Elizabeth for almost three months and then returned home.* Elizabeth's baby, John, would have been born either shortly before or shortly after Mary's departure. It is likely that Mary would have stayed for the birth and circumcision and joined the family in celebration before returning to her own home. Luke's account places John's birth and Mary's departure together.

John's circumcision occurs *on the eighth day* (1:59), as prescribed in Jewish law. Jesus' circumcision also occurs *on the eighth day* following his birth (2:21). Mary's time of purification was forty days (2:22; see also Leviticus 12), and it was at that time that Jesus was dedicated to the Lord as required of the first-born son with sacrifices made to "redeem" the child (2:22-24; see also Exodus 13). The sacrifice offered indicates the financial condition of the family (2:24; see also Leviticus 12:7b-8).

Other events in Jesus' life are dated: his visit to the temple at age twelve and the Feast of Passover (2:41-42). Jesus baptism occurred *in the fifteenth year of the reign of Tiberias Caesar* (3:1). Tiberias was emperor from AD 14-37, but had administrative authority as early as AD 4[23] and provincial authority by AD 11,[24] placing John's ministry historically, and locating Jesus' baptism as early as AD 25/26 but no later than AD 29/30. Luke does not give dates, but adds other verifiable historical detail here as well:

Pontius Pilate was governor of Judea AD 26-37.

> Herod Antipas was tetrarch of Galilee AD 4-39. The sons of Herod the Great–Archelaus, Antipas, and Philip–succeeded their father to rule a divided "kingdom" under the watchful eye of Rome.

> Herod Philip was tetrarch of Iturea and Trachonitis, and Lysanias was tetrarch of Abilene. No more is known of Lysanias, but Theophilus would likely have had the resources to confirm Luke's information.

> Annas and Caiaphas were high priests. Annas, Caiaphas' father-in-law, was high priest from AD 6 until AD 15 when he was deposed by Gratus, a Roman official.[25] His son,

---

[23] Grant, p 20

[24] NIV Study Bible footnote to Luke 3:1

[25] NIV Study Bible footnote to Luke 3:2

Eleazar, succeeded him for a couple
of years, and then Joseph Caiaphas
was high priest from AD 18-36.[26]

Eyewitnesses were important to the Apostle
Paul, as well. In recounting the early creed in 1
Corinthians 15, Paul lists the several post-resur-
rection appearance of Jesus, including one *to more
than five hundred of the brothers at the same time, most
of whom are still living...* (v. 6). The implication is
that the report can be verified by eyewitnesses.
One need only make contact with any of the living
witnesses to obtain an eyewitness account. At the
time Paul wrote this letter, Peter and most of the
Twelve were also still living. It would have been a
relatively simple matter for the readers of the letter
to confirm Paul's account.

Greek mythology (the people's religion)
included virgin births, incarnations, miracles, and
resurrections. Since the reports included a virginal
birth for Jesus, Luke needed to set it in Theophilus
mind as verifiable historical fact, attested by eyewitnesses. The miraculous birth of John is juxta-
posed because it is *not* virginal. Miracles, in Luke,
are witnessed and attested. The death of Jesus is
witnessed by a Roman centurion. But a real person
would not have miraculously appeared from
nowhere as an adult to teach and perform miracles. The nativity is a vital aspect of establishing
Jesus as a real person.

---

[26] James R. Edwards, *Is Jesus the Only Savior* (Grand
Rapids:Wm. B. Eerdmans, 2005), p 36.

Luke gives historical settings to details Matthew mentions, such as the birthplace of Jesus. Where Matthew has Jesus' birth in Bethlehem to fulfill prophecy, Luke places it there because of Caesar's edict. Luke includes the shepherds as witnesses because, presumably, they could be verified. *They spread the word concerning what had been told them about this child, and all who heard it were amazed at what the shepherds said to them* (2:17-18). People heard the shepherds talk about their experience with the angels and their visit to the birthplace.

Luke also includes a genealogy. But his is different in several ways from Matthew's genealogy. Because Matthew's concern is the prophecy-fulfilling Jewish Messiah and "son of David", he traces Jesus' genealogy through King David to Abraham. There is Jewish identity, tribal identity (Judah), and royal lineage. However, Joseph is descended through Jeconiah (Matthew 1:11-12, Jehoiachin, see 2 Kings 24:8-17; 2 Chronicles 36:9-10), being legal descent, while Mary was a descendant of King David's son Nathan (Luke 4:31; 2 Samuel 5:14), conferring biological descent. In contrast to Matthew, Luke traces Jesus' genealogy all the way back to Adam, connecting Jesus not just with the Jews, but with all mankind. He is thus not only the Savior of the Jews, but the Savior of the whole world. As a Gentile and companion of Paul, Luke no doubt shared Paul's deep concern for the mission to the Gentiles and their inclusion in the Body of Christ.

Luke's version of Jesus' genealogy is in the reverse order from Matthew's. Matthew begins with Abraham and ends with Jesus; Luke begins with Jesus and ends with *"Adam, the son of God."* There we discover that Jesus is not a son of the gods, but the son of God, a difference that is linguistically subtle but religiously astronomic. It is interesting that Luke's genealogy, ending with *"the son of Adam, the son of God"*, is placed immediately after the baptism, in which a voice from heaven declares of Jesus, *"You are my Son..."* (4:22).

Here, also, the careful reader will continue to observe Luke's meta-narrative, that Jesus was a real historical figure, whose life and deeds were witnessed and verifiable. One may be as sure of Jesus as of any other historical person, and the proofs of Jesus are as certain as they can be for any person in history. For Luke, Jesus' birth is a vital part of that historically-verified life – which also means that Jesus' miracles and teachings are credible.

John–the importance of deity

While John does not include a nativity narrative in his gospel, his meta-narrative makes his writing crucial to understanding Christmas. His purpose is found in 20:30-31, and indicates that John very carefully selected the events and sayings from Jesus' life to fit his purpose:

Jesus did many other miraculous signs in the presence of his disciples, which are not recorded in this book. But these are written that you may believe that Jesus is the Christ, the Son of God, and that by believing you may have life in his name.

John's plainly declares that Jesus is divine, that he is the Son of God. When we believe that, we *have life in his name*. Thus, it is not the birth of Jesus, per se, that is important, but the divine purpose for Jesus' coming, which is the focus of chapter one.

John reaches back in an echo of Genesis, *"In the beginning…"*, to set the stage for his narrative, and begins by identifying Jesus as God. In a free translation, John says, *"In the beginning the Word existed, and the Word was face-to-face with God, and God was the Word. He was face-to-face with God and is the agent of creation. He created all things, and everything that exists came into existence because of him"* (John 1:1-2). John thus identifies "the Word" as the Creator of Genesis 1. The Word and God, the God of the Old Testament (the Hebrew Scripture), are one and the same.

But this living God, this one beside whom there could be no other (Exodus 20:1-4; Deuteronomy 6:4-6), became human. John does not imply that Jesus is anything other than completely human. In fact, in his first letter, John sets Jesus' humanity as a "test of the spirits" – *This is how you can recognize the Spirit of God: Every spirit that acknowledges that Jesus Christ has come in the flesh is from God…* (1 John 4:2-3). The full humanity of Jesus is clearly on display throughout the Gospel, so John is not declaring that Jesus is some hybrid God-man, but that his essential nature was both fully human and fully divine. The import of this for those first Christians is often missed. We tend to forget that the first Christians were Jews. They kept kosher; they attended synagogue; they studied the Torah. And they wholeheartedly subscribed to the Shema: *"Hear, O Israel, the LORD our God is one…"* This one God was worthy of complete, undivided devotion.

Beside him there is no other. It was the height of blasphemy for a man to claim any sort of equality with God – or for anyone to claim such for another. The punishment for blasphemy was death – so this is a claim that we dare not take lightly. And yet, those early believers could conceive of no other way to describe Jesus.

Paul, who recorded the earliest creed discussed above, also shared an early church hymn:

> *Who, being in very nature God, did not consider equality with God something to be grasped, but made himself nothing* (or, *emptied himself*), *taking the very nature of a servant, being made in human likeness. And being found in appearance as a man he humbled himself and became obedient to death — even death on a cross!* (Philippians 2:6-8).

This hymn predates John's gospel, indicating that it was not John's letter that determined the early Christian theology.[27] Rather John reflects to us what the "primitive" church already believed.[28] The significance of this should not be lost to us: Paul prided himself on the purity of his Jewish heritage (Philippians 3:4-6), but was willing to sacrifice all of that for the sake of Christ. We understand that this "Hebrew of Hebrews" found the evidence for the deity of Jesus so overwhelming

---

[27] Paul wrote the letter to the Philippians c. AD 53-55, while the Gospel of John was composed perhaps as late as AD 85.

[28] See also Colossians 1:15-20 and Hebrews 1:1-4

that he had to find accommodation for it, even against everything he had grown up believing.

John does more than connect Jesus with the God of Creation. He goes on to place Jesus in the wilderness with Israel and the Exodus. While we use John 1:14 to support our theology of Incarnation, those few words contain much more than we see from our distance.

> *And the Word became flesh and dwelt among us, (and we have seen his glory, the glory as of the only begotten of the Father,) full of grace and truth* (KJV).

> *The Word became flesh and made his dwelling among us. We have seen his glory, the glory of the One and Only, who came from the Father, full of grace and truth* (NIV).

"Dwelt among" or "made his dwelling" would be better understood as "pitched his tent (tabernacle)". Using this phrase will help us understand what John is saying. And then, "among us" should be understood as "in our midst". So, a proper reading of this verse is –

> *The Word became flesh and pitched his tent in our midst. And we have seen his glory...*

During the Exodus, the tribal communities were camped with the Tabernacle in the center of the camp. According to Numbers 2, three camps each were camped to the north, south, east and west, and the Tabernacle in the middle, so that the focal point of their national life was the place of worship. In Exodus 25, the furnishings for the Tabernacle are ordered; then in chapter 26, the building of the Tabernacle itself is ordered. In chapter 40, the tabernacle is erected. That finished, the writer records: *Then the cloud covered the Tent of Meeting and the glory of the LORD filled the tabernacle* (Exodus 40:34). The Tabernacle, then, becomes not only the center of worship, but also the place of God's dwelling. God, symbolized by the pillar of cloud/fire, came to the center of the camp.

So, with 1:14, John intentionally connects Jesus with the Exodus and with the tabernacle of God's glory. He pitches a tent of flesh in our midst – in the center of the camp of humanity. Jesus not only takes on human flesh, but he does so in a way that reflects the very presence of God. John tells us that the Word is God with us, God in the flesh, and it is God's glory that covers the humanity of Jesus. Just as *the glory filled the tabernacle*, so with the enfleshment (or, Incarnation) of Jesus, *we have seen his glory, the glory of the One and Only, who came from the Father, full of grace and truth*. The parallel is striking – and meant to be.

John includes a reference to his meta-narrative in his first letter: *That which was from the beginning... which was with the Father and has appeared to us* (1 John 1:1-2).

So, while John included no nativity narrative, his account of Jesus' origin is crucial to the story of Christmas, and an integral part of the Christian celebration, perhaps being read as the conclusion to the Christmas "story". The careful reader, here again, will observe John's meta-narrative throughout the gospel.

So, how important is Christmas to the story of the Church? Should thoughtful Christians celebrate Christmas? If we base our answers on the gospels, their inclusion of the birth narratives and the reasons for their accounts, the answers will be in the affirmative. The birth narratives serve to place the man Jesus as a genuine historical figure and not the stuff of myth (Luke) and as the fulfillment of the Jewish messianic hope (Matthew). Matthew gives us Jesus, the Son of David. Luke gives us Jesus, the son of Man. John gives us Jesus the Christ, the Son of God. The birth narratives protect the Church, in some measure, from mythologizing Jesus so that he is too easily dismissed or ignored, because while similarities to myth are interesting the differences are profound. They also help us keep the delicate balance of the divine-human. While Matthew and Luke both affirm the humanity of the Messiah, John affirms his deity along with his humanity, both crucial elements of Christian orthodoxy. They also remind us that Jesus is the fulfillment of the Abrahamic covenant in which God promised to bless all nations through the offspring of Abraham. Jesus, via the birth narratives, fulfills God's pledge that the Jewish nation would be a kingdom of priests; that is, the intercessor between God and all of humanity.

It seems then, that as much as we might celebrate the death and resurrection of Jesus, we ought also to celebrate his birth. The Word become flesh, pitching his tabernacle in our midst, bringing the

glory of God to man, adds to rather than sub-
tracts from the significance of the passion and
resurrection. The nativities ground Jesus so that
the story of death and resurrection resist mythol-
ogization–grounding those events firmly in historical reality. There is no mysterious appearance
or departure, but the life of Jesus is witnessed and
proclaimed from beginning to end, and, with the
Ascension, beyond.

Whether such celebration occurs on December
25 or some other time of year is irrelevant. Whether
we know, or can know, with any degree of cer-
tainty, the precise date of Jesus' birth is irrelevant.
Whatever the historical Church has done to appro-
priate pagan or secular holidays is also irrelevant.
The gospel reminds us that Jesus, Son of David,
Son of Man, Son of God, the divine-human Christ,
was truly born, lived, died, and was raised from
the dead. The life of Jesus the Christ is worth celebrating from start to finish. And, while we may
focus our celebration to a single day, or short
season (such as Advent), we should not limit it
to that day or season, but find it relevant to every
day of our lives. The message of Christmas, as
the Advent of the Christ, is timeless and joyful,
and pulls us into the story of God's great work of
redemption and reconciliation.

Let the angelic message echo – *To you is born
this day a Savior, who is Christ the Lord.*

10

BAPTIZED

Mark 1:1-13; Matthew 3:13-17;
Luke 3:21-23a, John 1:19-36

L ENT IS A FORTY-DAY period during
which Christians recall and re-enact the forty
days of fasting Jesus spent in the desert. It
begins with his baptism and includes the fasting
and temptations, and then ends with Palm Sunday.
It is for the Church, for Christians, what Rosh
Hashanah and Yom Kippur are for the Jews. The
Jewish holy days, the Solemn Season, are shorter
in duration, being just ten days.

The Jewish calendar begins with Rosh
Hashanah, the Jewish New Year, and, as you might
expect, is also a season of rejoicing, parties, and celebration. But after the initial celebration, Jews are
called upon to reflect on their past year, to right
wrongs, restore relationships, repent of wrongdoing, and prepare themselves for Yom Kippur, the
Day of Atonement. Lent is supposed to also serve
that purpose for us. Many Christians will respond
to Lent by fasting, giving up something important

to them for these forty days. Some will skip a meal every day. Some will give up eating meat for the entire time. Some give up television or chocolate. It has also been a time for some to give up smoking or alcoholic beverage, and find healing from those habits. The idea behind the fasting is to remember that Jesus fasted forty days in the desert.

The events that inspire Lent begin with the baptism of Jesus. I remember asking, as a teenager, and not getting a satisfactory answer, why Jesus had to be baptized. You see, our view of baptism is based on the ministry of John the Baptist. In Acts 19, Paul asked the Ephesian church if they had received the Holy Spirit when they believed. They had not even heard of the Holy Spirit, *so Paul asked, "Then what baptism did you receive?"*

"John's baptism," they replied.

Paul said, "John's baptism was a baptism of repentance."... On hearing this, they were baptized into the name of the Lord Jesus (Acts 19:1-6). Different baptisms, John and Jesus, and thus different meanings. Mark 1:4 tells us that *John was preaching a baptism of repentance for the forgiveness of sins.* And that's been our view of baptism. Believer baptism, the kind we always do, is a baptism of repentance. One denomination describes baptism as "the sign and seal of the new covenant of grace". We recite the Apostles' Creed affirming our belief in Christ. We ask the candidate, "Do you acknowledge Jesus Christ as your personal Savior, and do you realize that He saves you now?"[29] And we view it as a sort of first

---

[29] ¶800.1. *The Baptism of Believers*, Manual of the Church of the Nazarene, 2013-2017 (Kansas City: Nazarene Publishing

step in our Christian journey – a sign of our repentance and forgiveness; a sign of our acceptance of God's grace in Jesus.

And because we view baptism through the lens of John's baptism, we are confused about why Jesus had to be baptized. In Matthew's account, John was reluctant to baptize Jesus. Even he didn't see the point. Matthew tells us that Jesus waded out into the river toward John to be baptized. *But John tried to deter him, saying, "I need to be baptized by you, and do you come to me?"* (Matthew 3:14). John understood that he was preaching and baptizing for repentance, for the forgiveness of sin. He understood that the sinful ought to be baptized by the righteous. He recognized that Jesus was righteous and that he, John, was a sinner. In a baptism of repentance, John would need to be baptized by Jesus. And here comes Jesus expecting to be baptized, and not to be the baptizer. John was as confused as we are.

The Scriptures tell us that Jesus was without sin. 1 Peter 2:22 – *He committed no sin, and no deceit was found in his mouth.* Jesus was *a lamb without blemish or defect* (1 Peter 1:19). *God made him who had no sin to be sin for us* (2 Corinthians 5:21). Jesus was *tempted in every way, just as we are, yet was without sin* (Hebrews 4:15).[30] So, if Jesus was sinless, why was he baptized? And why, in his own words, was it needed *to fulfill all righteousness* (Matthew 3:15)? The confusion comes because we are focused on John, and not on Jesus. And we

House, 2013), p. 246

[30] See also Acts 3:14; Hebrews 7:26; 1 John 3:5

are forgetting an important part of John's message and Jesus' mission.

Matthew 3:2 tells us that John was preaching, *"Repent, for the kingdom of heaven is near."* He is the one preparing the way for the Lord (Matthew 3:3[31]). Mark and Luke both quote Isaiah and tell us that John fulfilled the prophecy of the "forerunner". By the way, Israel in John's day, would have understood Isaiah's prophecy to refer to the one who arrived in a city to announce the imminent arrival of the king. The city needed to prepare; the local officials needed to put together a welcoming party, prepared to meet the king on his arrival. And John's gospel has the Baptizer answering his critics with the words of Isaiah, *"I am the voice of one calling in the desert, 'Make straight the way for the Lord'"* (John 1:23). The Baptizer understood that he was announcing the coming king, the one coming to assume the throne, and be acknowledged as Lord and Ruler. We focus on the call to repent and neglect the announcement of the Kingdom. We focus on our sin, and neglect our Savior.

What Jesus was doing, by his own words, was not about sin and repentance but about righteousness and the Kingdom. Jesus was not being baptized because he was a sinner, but because he was the Savior. If we listen to the words from the Voice from above, we'll know. When Jesus comes up out of the water (and it does not say how deep the water was), the Holy Spirit descends on him in the form of a dove. A Voice is heard: *"This is my*

---

[31] Isaiah 40:3

beloved Son in whom I am well-pleased." Those are the words of a king passing on the crown to the crown-prince. The baptism of Jesus is an anointing. He is the Anointed One, the promised Davidic king. In the words of the Old Testament, he is *Ha Mashiach*, the Anointed of God, the Messiah; in Greek, the Christ. In other words, Jesus' baptism is his enthronement, his crowning. Just as David was anointed by Samuel while Saul was yet king, and it was a few years before David could assume the throne, so Jesus is anointed. The *becoming king* is a process that will take some time. A triumphal entry is required, as well as a formal declaration of kingship. The Roman procurator, Pontius Pilatus, will have the honor of declaring, "This is the King of the Jews", as Jesus is crowned and exalted. But the world will not see it for what it is. They will see a crown of thorns, a scepter of bullrush, and a throne in the form of a cross.

There is also the significance of the place where Jesus was baptized. Tradition suggests that John chose the location where Joshua led Israel in to possess the land. After forty years of wilderness wandering, Israel had, for the second time, come to the borderlands of Promise. They had escaped Egyptian slavery by passing through the water of the Red Sea. We could compare that with John's baptism, and the idea of repentance and forgiveness of sin. Our baptism is that of slaves set free. But God never intended for Israel to simply escape Egypt. God did not take them into the wilderness because that's where he wanted them. The wilderness was not the destination. They were intended to escape Egypt and pass through the wilderness.

And, indeed, it was a short journey from Egypt to the place where they sent the twelve spies to check out their new home. But the spies, ten of the twelve, returned with a fearful report. Even the urging of the two could not sway the opinion of the people. They turned back in fear, condemned to wander.

That fearful generation died, all but two – Joshua and Caleb, the faithful spies with the good report – and Israel arrived at last, once more, at the borderland. A flood-stage river stood in their way. God repeated with Joshua what he had done forty years before with Moses, and opened a way through the river. Tribal elders were instructed to pick up stones from the river bed and build a memorial altar on the bank. This place, marked with a monument – this place of crossing over, is a significant place, and the likely location where the Baptizer set to work. John picked this place and the symbolism would not have been lost on those who heard John's message and came to him for baptism.

As John baptized, the people re-enacted their own crossing from the wilderness, a sort of reclamation of their history. But was this the place of repentance, of freedom from sin?

No, that was the Red Sea. That was the place people fled from slavery. That was the place of leaving; this was the place of entering. You see, Joshua led the people across the Jordan, not to leave but to enter. Yes, they were leaving the wilderness. Every entrance involves an exit – you leave one room to enter another. Far more importantly, though, they were entering the Land of

Promise. They were here to take possession. And every beginning involves an ending. This was a kind of ending – an end to the wilderness, and an end to the journey. But it was really a beginning. It was the beginning of their life as a people with a place. It was the beginning of a new life and a new national identity.

There's one more thing significant here that we shouldn't miss. It's the similarity in names. We miss it because of the way we've translated the Bible, and because of the way we understand it. Joshua, Yeshua, is the Hebrew form of the name; Jesus, ΊhsoØς (Iesous), is the Greek form of the same name. Jesus, *Yeshua*, is re-enacting the thing that Joshua, *Yeshua*, did so many years before. He is leading the way into the Kingdom. Jesus is none other than the King, come to establish his Kingdom, and here at the river, leading the way, taking the first steps toward the answer to the Kingdom prayer that he was to teach the disciples – *Thy kingdom come; thy will be done on earth as it is in heaven* (Matthew 6:10).

As Jesus steps into the waters he is not leaving a life of sin, for he has no such life to leave. As Jesus steps into the waters of baptism, he is leading the way into a new life, the life of the Kingdom. This is that first step, by the way, that confused Nicodemus so much. For when Jesus told Nicodemus that the new birth from above required a birth of water... Well, here's what Jesus actually said, *"I tell you the truth, no one can enter the kingdom of God unless he is born of water and the Spirit"* (John 3:5). Just as Israel could not enter the Promised Land without passing through the river, so Christian baptism is the "crossing of the river" to enter the Kingdom of God. Thus, when Jesus told Nicodemus that the new birth from above required a birth of water he was speaking of the waters of baptism, not the crossing of the Red Sea but the crossing of the Jordan.

You see, our problem has been that, for us, baptism has been the crossing of the Red Sea, the leaving of slavery to sin. That's the baptism of John. The baptism of Jesus, the baptism into the name of Jesus that Paul spoke of to Ephesus in Acts 19, is the crossing of the Jordan, the entry into the new life, the entry into the Kingdom. It is not the mere escape from slavery, but the entry into freedom in Christ.

And so Jesus responded to John's objection, *"Let it be so now; it is proper for us to do this to fulfill all righteousness."* Jesus led the way through the waters of freedom, and inaugurated his Kingdom – and invites us to follow.

11

DRIVEN BY THE SPIRIT

Luke 4:1-13; Matthew 4:1-11; Mark 1:12-13

I WAS ASKED A QUESTION relating to the work of the Holy Spirit in our lives. It was about the word often translated *perfection*, and the concept of "Christian perfection." The best resource is John Wesley's pamphlet titled "A Plain Account of Christian Perfection", in which he has compiled sermons, letters, and conference notes on the subject. Wesley was not ashamed to use the term because it was in the Bible, but he did feel the need to explain and defend it in the face of so much misunderstanding. There are a couple things we also need to understand:

First, there is a problem with translation. In about AD 384, St. Jerome translated the Greek New Testament into Latin, then the common, or *vulgar*, language of the people. The form of Greek used is called *koine*, or common, Greek, and the Latin word for common is *vulgar*. So Jerome's translation was called the Vulgate, or common Latin translation. But Greek doesn't translate well into

Latin any more than it does into English. Where the Greek used the word *telios*, Jerome translated with the Latin *perfectus*. Though it is probably the best choice, it has a much different connotation in English: *perfectus* implies flawlessness or free of error, a more Western view of perfection. But *telios* has to do with maturity, completion, and being "perfectly suited to a task". A tool or machine that does what it was designed to do could be said to be *telios*, perfect, so the word applies to one who fulfills the function for which they were designed. Newer Bible translations have rendered *telios* as mature or complete rather than perfect.

Second, Wesley felt it necessary to explain what "Christian perfection" was not. Among the things that it is not is any sort of flawlessness, as if we were angelic, or like Adam before the fall, who still, by the way, managed to sin. We still make mistakes because we simply don't have perfect knowledge. We don't have perfect judgment. With all the best and most noble of intentions we still screw up. In other words, sanctification does not eliminate our humanity. It does not take away the problem of temptation, and it does not take away our ability to sin. What the Holy Spirit does do, though, is give us the power to resist temptation, and the ability to not sin. The danger for us is to believe that sanctification makes us, in any sense, flawless. "Perfect" is the wrong word for us because it just carries way too much baggage. As we know all too well, no one is perfect.

This is important because the focus of this chapter is the work of the Holy Spirit in the life of Jesus. We also need to face a couple more problems: First, a lot of Christians seem to think that the Holy Spirit came into being at Pentecost. I hear people talk about the Holy Spirit being "given" or "poured out" at Pentecost, as if it had never happened before; as if the Holy Spirit was something brand new at the moment. The Holy Spirit, by the way, is not "it" but "he", not a force or power, but a person. He is the Third Person of the Triune Godhead, existing with God for all eternity, as theologians say, "Co-eternal and co-existent." And the Holy Spirit is active throughout the Bible, appearing to us in the very first verses of Genesis. Genesis 1:2 relates that *the Spirit of God was hovering over the waters.*

For example, Moses and seventy elders had the Spirit on them (Exodus 11:17, 25). Bezalel, who was to construct the articles for the Tabernacle in the wilderness, was filled with the Spirit of God (Exodus 31:3). The judges Othniel (Judges 3:10), Gideon (Judges 6:34), Jephthah (Judges 11:29) and Samson (Judges 14:6, 19); the kings Saul (1 Samuel 10:10) and Azariah (2 Chronicles 15:1; the prophet Jehaziel (2 Chronicles 20:14) and the priest Zechariah (2 Chronicles 24:20) are all described as having been filled with the Holy Spirit at one point in their lives. In the New Testament, Luke's nativity account includes the prophecy that John the Baptist would be filled with the Holy Spirit from birth (Luke 1:15), that Elizabeth, on hearing Mary's greeting, was filled with the Holy Spirit (Luke 1:41) and that Zechariah's prophecy came when he was filled with the Holy Spirit (Luke 1:67). Someone with more time would discover many more such instances in both the Old and New Testaments occurring prior to Pentecost.

Second, we have a rather benign view of the Holy Spirit. I've heard well-meaning but thoroughly misinformed (or deluded) people equate the Holy Spirit to the "feminine side" of God, or the "feminine aspect of the divine". There is no Scriptural warrant for that, but it seems to be a way of taming God. That is, the Holy Spirit is there to bless us, to protect us, to give us stuff – like spiritual gifts. His job, it appears, is to make us happy, to comfort us, to teach us, to help us to be good and holy. The problem with that is that it is partly true, but only partly.

It's like saying that God is love. Of course he is, and there are plenty of Scriptures to back that up. But that's not *all* that God is. God is also holy, just, and–the theological three–all-powerful, all-wise, and ever-present. God is love, of course, but not with a wimpy, permissive, tolerant love. He loves you enough to make you uncomfortable with sin, enough to apply consequences to sin, enough to discipline you and change you.

So when Jesus promised the Holy Spirit to the disciples in John 14-16, he describes him as paravklhton (parakleton), using a compound word that means "one who is called alongside." The word is translated *Comforter* (KJV), *Counselor* (NIV), or *Advocate* (1 John 2:1). Then Jesus says, the Holy Spirit *"will teach you all things..."* (John 14:26), and describes him as *the Spirit of truth* (John 15:26) who *"will guide you into all truth* (John 16:13). The work of the Holy Spirit is to *"convict the world of guilt in regard to sin and righteousness and judgment..."* (John

16:8), and to *"bring glory to"* Jesus (John 16:14). Then Jesus said, *"you will receive power when the Holy Spirit comes on you..."* (Acts 1:8), implying that the Holy Spirit is the source of our ability to testify to the work of Christ, the source of our ability to be witnesses. Thus, the work of the Holy Spirit IS to comfort us, to teach us, to give us power to live a righteous life. But that's not all he does, and we see that in the moment after Jesus' baptism.

Two things happen in quick succession following Jesus' anointing by John the Baptist: One, *the Holy Spirit descended on him in bodily form like a dove* (Luke 3:22), which is where we get the idea of representing the Holy Spirit with a dove. In human terms, this is when we might suggest that Jesus was "filled with the Holy Spirit". Some heresies suggest that it was this moment when Jesus becomes divine, becomes "the Christ". No, remember this carefully – Jesus was *always* divine, the Word become flesh to dwell with us (John 1:14). Jesus is the eternal Word, again co-equal and co-eternal with the Father and the Spirit, and, in our list, the Second Person of the Triune Godhead. Whatever you want to call it, though, here Jesus is empowered for his ministry. But first, before he can begin, the second thing must happen.

Matthew and Luke tell us that Jesus was *led by the Spirit into the desert* (Matthew 4:1; Luke 4:1), but Mark is much more emphatic: *At once the Spirit sent him out into the desert* (Mark 1:12). Matthew 14:22 tells us that Jesus *made* the disciples get into the boat that was headed into the storm. Sometimes we are led; sometimes we are sent. God has more for us than a wishy-washy sheltered faith. Hebrews 12: 6 says that *the Lord disciplines those he loves*. God wants us to grow; he wants us to mature, to become complete and "perfectly suited to the task". Sometimes God shelters us from the storms and sometimes he sends us into the storms.

There is a difference between the followers of Jesus and the disciples of Jesus. There are those who merely follow, who merely believe. But I want to be a disciple, an imitator, of Jesus. The word *disciple* means *one who is under discipline*. It is more than a student; a disciple is one who intends not only to learn from his teacher, but also to become like his teacher. The purpose of discipline is to form our character and make us mature.

Hebrews 5:8-9 says, *Although he was a son, he learned obedience from what he suffered and, once made perfect* (there's that word again!), *he became the source of eternal salvation for all who obey him...*

Jesus' time in the wilderness is not accidental, or even voluntary. He is sent, in a sense, driven, into the desert – but not as an exile. As we told the story of the meta-narrative, we suggested that Jesus re-enacted events from the Old Testament. He was identifying himself with the nation. His baptism was a re-enactment of the crossing of the Jordan by Joshua to enter and claim the land of Promise. After Israel had left Egypt and experienced their baptism of deliverance in the crossing of the Red Sea, they went directly to the boundary of that land, but turned back in fear. God sentenced them to forty years in the wilderness. In a sense, they fasted, because what they ate was provided by God: water from a rock and from a stagnant pool sweetened with a tree branch; quail blown in on the wind; and manna, an interesting description roughly equivalent to "whatchama-callit", sometimes called "bread from heaven". Now Jesus re-enacts the wilderness wanderings with his own forty days fasting in the wilderness. His job, as he declared to John, is *to fulfill all righteousness*. Jesus must become Israel, identify fully with them, take upon himself all that they are. Paul wrote, *God made him who had no sin to be sin for us, so that in him we might become the righteousness of God* (2 Corinthians 5:21). Jesus had to become fully one of us so that he could fully represent us in the grand work of salvation.

But Jesus' purpose in the desert was not merely to represent Israel, or to re-enact Israel's spiritual history. Mark says that Jesus *was in the desert forty days being tempted by Satan* (Mark 1:13). Luke agrees: Jesus was *in the desert, where for forty days he was tempted by the devil* (Luke 4:2). Matthew, however, says that Jesus was *in the desert **to be** tempted by the devil. And after fasting forty days and forty nights, he was hungry.* [Then] *the tempter came to him...* (Matthew 4:1-3). That is, after the period of fasting, when Jesus was at his weakest, came the time of testing. I suspect I'd have been tempted to turn stones to bread a long time before the forty days was up. Matthew's version of the story implies that Satan came to him when Jesus was weak, when Jesus was most humanly vulnerable. But Jesus was there on purpose.

Two more things occur to me in this context: Moses spent forty years in the wilderness before his burning bush encounter with God, and before he led Israel out of slavery.

Then this from Leviticus 16: this chapter describes the ritual of Yom Kippur, the Day of Atonement. Part of that ritual involved two goats. One of them was to be sacrificed as a sin offering. The other was to be a "scapegoat". *Scape* is an archaic term for a means of escape or a small mistake of forgetfulness. The high priest, in this case, Aaron, was to *lay both hands on the head of the live goat and confess over it all the wickedness and rebellion of the Israelites – all their sins – and put them on the goat's head* (Leviticus 16:21). The goat was then taken some distance away from the camp and released into the wilderness; it was not killed in sacrifice. *The goat will carry on itself all their sins to a solitary place* (Leviticus 16:22). In this way, the "wickedness and rebellion" of Israel and all their sins was symbolically separated from them, and sent away from them. Thus, Israel escaped punishment – the goat was a "way of escape" (see 1 Corinthians 10:13). And God would forget their sins. In Jeremiah 31:34, God says, *"For I will forgive their wickedness and will remember their sins no more"* – the goat was "a mistake of forgetfulness" (see also Hebrews 8:12; 10:17).

I have begun to see echoes of the Old Testament story now whenever I read the New Testament. I see the Old being re-enacted, answered, and fulfilled in the New. And here, I see, not only the symbolism of the forty days in the wilderness, but the Christ being driven into the wilderness – re-enacting the passing through the water, identifying with Israel, and then begin sent into the wilderness. It makes me believe that God was re-enacting, or fulfilling in Jesus, the function of the scapegoat.

When we begin to make these sorts of connections, there are other things that point that way. As Israel confessed their sins over the head of the scapegoat, so the concept of confession is repeated in the New Testament in relation to faith in Jesus. Paul writes, *if you confess with your mouth, "Jesus is Lord," and believe in your heart that God raised him from the dead, you will be saved* (Romans 10:9). And John: *If we confess our sins, he is faithful and just and will forgive us our sins and purify us from all unrighteousness* (I John 1:9). And the verse I quoted earlier: *God made him who had no sin to be sin for us, so that in him we might become the righteousness of God* (2 Corinthians 5:21). Jesus, then, became our scapegoat, our means of escape, and our assurance of God's forgetfulness.

It's important for us to understand, then, two things: One, Jesus' forty days in the wilderness is not a "passing the time" sort of thing. It's not incidental to the story. It's an integral part of the story, particularly as it relates to Jesus identity as the Word become flesh – as it relates to Jesus humanity and identification with us.

And two: God may send us into the wilderness in some sense. The Holy Spirit may take us, or send us, or drive us, to places we don't want to go. He may send us to desert places, to difficult places, to dangerous places. The work of the Holy Spirit is not all "peaches and cream". We may be exactly where God wants us – and feel abandoned, lonely, and afraid. We may be sick, injured, set aside for a time – and still be in the center of God's will. It may be hard for us to understand, but the Comforter is not interested in your comfort, your ease, your peace and safety. He wants you to be holy, to be mature and "perfectly suited to the task". He wants you to be a testimony of grace. He wants you to be a blessing and a witness.

If you are going through tough times today, let me assure you: God has not forgotten you. He may have you right where he needs you to be. He can give meaning to your pain and suffering, more than you know. Through hardship, God is either preparing you for service or using you as a testimony of his love and grace. Jesus was sent into the wilderness for a purpose – and so are we.

12

BREAD IN THE WILDERNESS

Matthew 4:1-11; Exodus 16:1-36;
Deuteronomy 8:3-5, 15-18

A RE YOU WHERE YOU want to be in life? What do you need to do to grow and mature? What is the wilderness into which the Spirit has led or sent you? What testing are you facing, and what tools do you need to get through that time of testing? In the Church liturgical calendar, Lent is the season of remembering Jesus' temptation. As we spend the time contemplating Jesus' time in the wilderness, his example may help us as we face temptation..

Hebrews 4:15 tells us that Jesus was *tempted in every way, just as we are – yet was without sin.* Disagreements are sometimes raised, citing specific temptations–such as: was Jesus ever tempted to rob a bank? Was Jesus ever tempted by lust? Was Jesus ever tempted to do drugs? Those are diversions from the real issue. The point the author is making is not that Jesus faced the same temptations that you or I might, but that he faced the same *kinds* of temptations–temptations regarding personal appetites (hunger), lust for power, popularity, and fame. But the writer to the Hebrews wants us to know something more important than that Jesus faced temptation — he also wants us to know that Jesus was victorious. He did not yield to the temptations.

Even more to the point is that, through his temptations, Jesus came to identify with our condition. Paul wrote to the church at Corinth: *No temptation has seized you except what is common to man. And God is faithful; he will not let you be tempted beyond what you are able to bear. But when you are tempted, he will also provide a way out so that you may stand up under it* (1 Corinthians 10:13). The King James Version ends the verse this way:... *but will with the temptation also make a way to escape.*

Some are fond of saying that God will not give us more than we can handle. Not true. God often gives us much more than we can handle alone, but never more than he can handle on our behalf. God's desire is a relationship with us and that we will be part of his restored kingdom. To that end, we are learning faith. We are learning to trust God and to lean on his strength and wisdom. We are cast into deep water so that we depend upon God. We are given tasks and problems beyond our own strength, wisdom, and ability, so that God can work in our behalf. As with the story of Gideon, God chooses to work through the weak and unlikely so that his own strength is made apparent.

Temptation is common to our humanity. That is one thing we learn from the example of Jesus.

He was tempted, identifying with the human condition, but also showing us the way out, the way to victory. Temptation itself is not sin, and we do not sin by being tempted; we sin when we give in to the temptation. But God provides us with an escape hatch when temptations come.

But there is more to Jesus' temptations than just identifying with the human condition. Let's take a look at them, beginning with the first.

> *Then Jesus was led by the Spirit into the desert to be tempted by the devil. After fasting forty days and forty nights, he was hungry. The tempter came to him and said, "If you are the Son of God, tell these stones to become bread"* (Matthew 4:1-3).

We've already mentioned the significance of the forty days–one day for every year that Israel wandered in the wilderness between Egyptian slavery and the Promised Land. There is, at least on Matthew's part, a clear attempt to identify Jesus with Israel. But we need to dig a bit deeper here. For that, we go to Deuteronomy 8:3-5.

Deuteronomy, a Greek word meaning "second law", was Moses' last message to Israel before his death and before the nation crossed the Jordan to take possession of the Land of Promise. He reminded them of their slavery and the long journey they had nearly completed. Among the many "blessings" of their wilderness experience was this: *"[God] humbled you, causing you to hunger and then feeding you with manna, which neither you* nor your fathers had known, to teach you that man does not live on bread alone but on every word that comes from the mouth of God. Your clothes did not wear out and your feet did not swell during these forty years. Know then in your heart that as a man disciplines his son, so the LORD your God disciplines you."

If you continue reading in Matthew, you already know Jesus' answer to Satan – Matthew 4:4: *Jesus answered, "It is written: 'Man does not live on bread alone, but on every word that comes from the mouth of God.'"*

Remember the words of Hebrews 5:8 – *Although he was a son, he learned obedience from what he suffered.* Connect that with Hebrews 12:5, where the author identifies Jesus' suffering and discipline with our own, in a quote from Proverbs 3:11-12 – *My son, do not make light of the Lord's discipline, and do not lose heart when he rebukes you, because the Lord disciplines those he loves, and he punishes everyone he accepts as a son.* Jesus' familiarity with the Deuteronomy story, that he quoted it in the moment of temptation, indicates to us that he was familiar with the last part of that as well – *Know then in your heart that as a man disciplines his son, so the LORD your God disciplines you.*

What that means, then, is that we ought to not view temptation as an evil thing, but that we see it as testing and prodding toward maturity. It means that we do not view hardship or suffering as God having abandoned us, but as God loving us and disciplining us. We need to understand that discipline is not necessarily punishment. There is that, but any discipline, such as practicing the piano, training for a marathon, learning any skill, may involve suffering as a means to maturity, a developed skill, and winning a race. According to an African proverb, "Smooth seas do not make skillful sailors." Discipline is required in any sport.

I took a group of children to a miniature golf course. One little boy couldn't hit the ball straight to save his life (so to speak), and he was jealous of another child who won a free ticket by hitting the ball into the last hole. I reminded him that Tiger Woods did not win a trophy the first time he played golf. He did not win the first game he played. Or the second. Or the third. His dad took him to the golf course and *disciplined* him – not punished him – in the game of golf. He practiced every day. Michael Jordan, Kobe Bryant, and LeBron James were not basketball stars the first time they picked up a ball. They had to learn the skills, practice, and be disciplined in the game of basketball. None of us are perfect Christians from the moment of salvation. We all slip and fall. Temptation is common, and discipline is necessary. We must practice our faith.

Christians should stop viewing suffering as punishment, as consequences for having displeased God. *Consider it pure joy, my brothers, whenever you face trials of many kinds, because you know that the testing of your faith develops perseverance. Perseverance must finish the work so that you may be mature and complete, not lacking anything* (James 1:2-4).

Now, back to the bread. Jesus' answer is based on the experience of Israel as recounted for us in Exodus 16.

Israel had just experienced an overwhelmingly powerful miracle of deliverance: passing through the Red Sea on dry ground. Some skeptical theologians claim that they actually crossed a swampy region known as the Sea of Reeds. Would that not be an even greater miracle – to think that the Egyptian army drowned in a swamp?

Exodus 15 is the victory song. Their song of rejoicing over their deliverance had barely ended before they started griping, complaining, grumbling, mumbling, murmuring, and whining about being hungry. They complained to Moses, "You just brought us out here to die because the Egyptian cemeteries were full." They had fled Egypt with unleavened bread, probably similar to what is now called matzoh, and when it ran out, they were hungry. They apparently thought it was up to Moses to feed them. From the Red Sea they had traveled three days before they found water, but the water they found was bitter. By a miracle it became sweet and they were able to quench their thirst. They then moved to an oasis called Elim where there was fresh water, but still no food.

As the people griped and grumbled, God told Moses that he would feed the people – meat in the evening and bread in the morning. But the bread came with some specific rules – they were to collect only what they needed for each day, and on the sixth day enough extra for the Sabbath because there would be no bread given on the seventh day. Do we hear echoes in Jesus' Kingdom Prayer? *"Give us this day our daily bread"* (Matthew 6:11).

True to God's word, *that evening quail came and covered the camp, and in the morning there was a layer of dew around the camp. When the dew was gone, thin flakes like frost on the ground appeared on the desert floor. When the Israelites saw it, they said to each other,"What is it?" For they did not know what it was* (Exodus 16:13-15). The name they gave the stuff was *manna*, which means "what is it?" Theologians and scientists have been trying to figure it out ever since. What was it? *Manna* is a question, not an answer. Moses gave them the answer, *"It is the bread the LORD has given you to eat."* It is your daily bread where there is no bread. It is God's daily gift to you, the gift of daily sustenance, daily life. In the desert, God provides.

There are two things about this story that Jesus knew: First, God is perfectly able to provide for all our needs. Jesus would try to get his people to understand that in the "sermon on the mount" – *"Therefore I tell you, do not worry about your life, what you will eat or drink"* (Matthew 6:25). Matthew recounts two feeding miracles in quick succession – the feeding of the five thousand (Matthew 14:13-20) and the feeding of the four thousand (Matthew 15:29-39). Jesus teaches and illustrates that God is able to provide for our needs. He teaches and illustrates that God cares about us enough to take care of us. The God who feeds birds and clothes flowers also feeds and clothes us. God's power, God's love, God's attention to us should never be in question. *"If you then, though you are evil, know how to give good gifts to your children, how much more will your Father in heaven give good gifts to those who ask him!"* (Matthew 7:11).

Jesus also knew that God could be trusted. God is always true to his word. Genesis tells us that it God spoke the world into existence,[32] that by his word that stars and planets spin in space, that light and darkness, summer and winter, birds and flowers even exist. God's word is powerful. In the desert God promised meat in the evening and bread in the morning. True to his word, there was. If God is leading us, God knows the way. "My Lord knows the way through the wilderness – all I have to do is follow."[33]

Talk show host Rush Limbaugh is fond of saying, "Words mean things." Other than our North American and European post-Enlightenment cultures, the rest of the world also believes that words mean things. Words have power. Anyone who has been verbally abused knows the power of words. Words have the power to change lives, the power to give life, and the power to kill. Words have the power to make us better or break us into pieces. The more power or influence a person has in our life, the more power their words have. A parent or teacher praises us and we blossom. They curse us, calling us "stupid", or making us feel worthless, and we wilt. By virtue of who he is, God's word is powerful. God's word means something. God's word feeds us, clothes us, gives us life, charges our faith.

---

[32] I am not here attempting to argue a scientific theory of creation, but only to respond to the Biblical account.

[33] My Lord Knows the Way, Words and Music by Sidney E. Cox , © 1951 Singspiration/ASCAP. All rights reserved, Used by permission of Brentwood-Benson Music Publishing, Inc.

Then Jesus was led by the Spirit into the desert to be tempted by the devil. After fasting forty days and forty nights, he was hungry. The tempter came to him and said, "If you are the Son of God, tell these stones to become bread" (Matthew 4:1-3). The tempter tried to make Jesus doubt who he was, tried to get him to rely on his own resources. Jesus refuses to fall for it, remembers Israel in the wilderness, and responds with Moses' encouraging words, *Jesus answered, "It is written: 'Man does not live on bread alone, but on every word that comes from the mouth of God.'"* (Matthew 4:4). He not only feeds our bodies, but he feeds our spirits as well. *In the beginning was the Word... in him was life, and that life was the light of men* (John 1:1-4). *Then Jesus declared, "I am the bread of life. He who comes to me will never go hungry"* (John 6:35). *"The words that I have spoken to you are spirit and they are life"* (John 6:63b). Jesus not only identified with us, but he also reminded us that God is faithful, and in him we live.

13

NOW, ABOUT THE RAPTURE...

ONE YEAR ON VACATION, I visited a church were I was guest speaker in the morning and just a guest in the evening. The moderator for the evening was showing a series of video lectures on the Second Coming of Christ. When discussion time came, the moderator, knowing my stance, asked, "Does anyone here not believe in the Rapture?" I silently raised my hand. Another lady, with a long history in our denomination whipped around in shock, "I don't believe it!" she declared, "A Nazarene pastor who doesn't believe in the Rapture!"

For clarity, let me state that I do not believe in a *secret* Rapture, for reasons that will be discussed later in this chapter. I do, however, believe strongly in the Second Coming of Christ. Perhaps we will have rapturous joy at the return of Christ, but that is not what is usually meant by "the Rapture". The Rapture is the concept that, at some point in a time of tribulation (referred to as The Great Tribulation), Jesus will return to snatch his people out of the world, thus sparing them the end times suffering to be experienced by everyone else. The catastrophes and judgments of the book of Revelation are then interpreted within this framework. Rapture theology is part and parcel of a pre-, mid-, post-Tribulation millennial controversy, and the date-setting and calendar-making of end times theologians. I have no interest in taking any position along the spectrum and defending it. As far as I am concerned, the whole structure is built on shaky ground and problematic interpretations of Scripture.

There are a number of problems with "rapture theology". Five are crucial to the thinking Christian:

1. Rapture theology is, like it or not, based on a gnostic cosmology that permeates much of what are loosely known as "eastern" religions. The Taoist dualism of yin/yang, good/evil, black/white, male/female is a near kin. This view is that nature, or the material world, is evil, created by an evil demiurge, and that spirit is good. That means that, as Christians, our hope is to escape this evil world for the good world of God's "heaven". Rapture theology, then, boils down to an escapist theology that appears nowhere in the Bible.

It also assumes a three-level universe, with hell beneath, heaven above, and the earth sandwiched between. Contrary to many interpretations, when Paul asserts that he knew a man who was *caught up to the third heaven* (2 Corinthians 12:2), he was not talking about a place, but about a state of ecstacy, a visionary experience, in which he saw and heard "inexpressible things." On Colossians 3:4, *"When Christ, who is your life, appears, then you also will appear with him in glory,",* N. T. Wright comments,

> "When we talk of Jesus coming, we make it sound as though he is presently far away: as though, to come, he would have to make a lengthy journey. But *appear* is different. As we find in many passages of the New Testament, Jesus is not far away; he is in heaven, and *heaven is not a place in the sky, but rather God's dimension of what we think of as ordinary reality....* heaven is not a place in our space-time continuum, but a different sphere of reality that overlaps and interlocks with our sphere in numerous though mysterious ways. It is as though there were a great invisible curtain hanging across a room..."[34]

Rapture theology misses God's many declarations in Genesis 1 that creation was both "good" and "very good." Dismissing the goodness and beauty of creation leads to a misunderstanding of such writings as Romans 8, which will be discussed later in this chapter. It also leads to despair and disregard for the world in which we live. Why take care of something that is about to be destroyed anyway? Why not take advantage of the resources

---

[34] N. T. Wright, *Surprised by Scripture*, p 96, emphasis his.

of the earth? The movement to preserve and protect endangered species, to recycle and reuse limited resources, and to care for the environment seem at odds with the idea that an evil, or disfigured, creation is about to be destroyed. "This world is not my home, I'm just a-passin' through", so why bother with it?

2. Rapture theology is, like it or not, based on misunderstanding, misinterpretation, and misuse of **three important and very valuable words** which are often used interchangeably, as if they mean the same thing. They don't. Theologians sometimes uses words that obscure or confuse the average Christian (whatever that means). We are sometimes afraid of such words, but we do not need to be.

> A. *Parousia* is a good theological word which means "appearing". It is sometimes used to refer to the "Second Coming", but that's incorrect–in the sense in which "Second Coming" is normally used. "The word, *parousia,* 'royal appearing,' was regularly used to describe Caesar's 'coming' or 'royal appearing' when visiting a city, or when returning home to Rome."[35]
>
> B. *Apocalypse* does not mean "catastrophe", in spite of the

---

[35] Wright, *Surprised by Scripture*, p. 101

common Hollywood usage in such films as the Vietnam war classic, "Apocalypse Now", or any of the other disaster movies. It does not mean "the end of the world" or even "the end of the world as we know it." *Apocalypse* really has little or nothing to do with "the end". *Apocalypse* means simply "unveiling" or "revelation", the title we've wrongly given to a book of the Bible: "The Revelation of St. John the Divine". Books of the Bible are often named by the first word (or words) of the book. In this case, the first words are, "The revelation of Jesus Christ". It is the *revealing* of Jesus, or the *unveiling* of Jesus, and Jesus is the central figure throughout. The subject of the Revelation is not the Beast, the Antichrist, the Millennium Reign, or the end of the world. It is not about what happens to Christians – it is always and forever about Jesus. Rapture theology forgets that.

C. Rapture theology also misuses the word *eschatology*, loosely translated "last things." But Jesus, in Matthew's eschatological discourse (Matthew 24-25), is not talking about the "end of time", but of the "end of the age", a rather obscure reference for which we really have no good definition. The events of Matthew 24-25 appear to have been mostly fulfilled in the fall of Jerusalem in AD 70. The *eschaton*, then, is not the end of the world, but the end of the present order – and those are two very different things.

3. A third problem with Rapture theology is the assumption that Christians are to be spared the suffering of tribulation and martyrdom. That is wishful thinking. Even as I write this, martyrdom is very real in some parts of the world. A recent news article reported that, in the year 2016, as many as 90,000 Christians were killed for their faith and another 600 million were prevented from practicing their faith.[36] On Palm Sunday of 2017, two Coptic churches in Egypt were bombed by anti-Christian terrorists, killing 45 worshipers and wounding more than 100. The truth is that Christians are not spared suffering in this world. Jesus himself declared that *"in this world you will have trouble..."* (John 16:33).

4. Rapture Theology ignores history, particularly that of First Century Israel, the historical context of Revelation, and the history of Christian persecution in the Roman Empire, particularly under the emperors Nero, Vespasian, Titus, and Domitian. For example, many of Jesus' prophecies in the last

---

[36] http://www.foxnews.com/world/2017/01/06/christians-most-persecuted-group-in-world-for-second-year- study.html

few chapters of Matthew were fulfilled in AD 70 when Jerusalem was sacked and burned by the Roman army under the command of Titus Flavius Vespasianus, the son of the emperor Vespasian.

History can provide valuable insight and correctives to our understanding of Biblical prophecy. In 334 BC, Alexander the Great invaded the Persian Empire and took possession of what we call the Holy Land in 333. When he died ten years later, the Greek Empire was divided among his generals. His successors established power blocks, two of which are important for us: the Egyptian Ptolemies and the Mesopotamian Seleucids. Judea was the "knot" in their tug-of-war. Eventually, the Seleucids gained a permanent upper hand. In 167 BC, the Seleucid king Antiochus IV Epiphanes desecrated the temple in Jerusalem, sacrificing pigs on the altar and setting up a statue to the Greek god Zeus. Antiochus also banned circumcision and other Jewish practices, including the speaking of Hebrew, and ordered that the Scriptures be translated into Greek. The product of this order was the Septuagint, so named because it was seventy Jewish scholars who translated the Hebrew Scriptures into Greek. This bears a striking resemblance to the prophecies of Daniel 11 (and may have fulfilled them) regarding struggle between the "king of the North" and the "king of the South", and the "abomination of desolation." Ignorance of history can cause us to misunderstand and distort the Scripture. The context of Biblical prophecy must also include the secular history that surrounds it.

5. Rapture theology ignores the unity and general message of the Bible. Rapture theologians engage in a "cut and paste" approach to the Bible, taking bits and pieces from Daniel, Isaiah, Ezekiel, Matthew, Revelation, and various of Paul's letters. They lift verses out of their literary, historical, and cultural context and attempt to reassemble them into a coherent end-times calendar, in what I describe as "blender" theology. Several of such theologians have taken this approach to its logical conclusion and tried to set the date of Christ's return, in direct violation of Jesus' own statement that, *"It is not for you to know the times or dates the Father has set by his own authority"* (Acts 1:7). No one knows the date or the hour (Matthew 24:36).

A member of a previous pastorate wrote, "After reading 1 Thessalonians 4:17, I believe in the rapture of the church." I responded to her and she began to ask questions. My response was essentially, "It's not what you think." Let's put 1 Thessalonians 4:17 into the context of other verses often used to support a Rapture theology.

> **1 Thessalonians 4:17** – *"After that, we who are still alive and are left* (perileipovmenoi–the remaining ones) *will be caught up together with them in the clouds to meet the Lord in the air. And so we will be with the Lord forever."*

There are several issues that need to be clarified with this verse. The first issue is the phrase *"we who are still alive and are left..."* Paul has just written in verse 15 this exact phrase: *"we who are alive and are left... will certainly not precede those who have fallen asleep."* Paul is making a point about the process of the Lord's return: those who have died in Christ will rise first, that is, they will be resurrected to life. The dead will be raised to life. Then those of us who are alive, that is, those of us who have not died, will join the resurrected ones to meet the Lord.

Rapture theology tries to have the "left behind" both ways. In 1 Thessalonians, it is those Christians who remain alive on the earth. But in Matthew 24, Christians are supposed to have been "taken", and those who are "left behind" are the unbelievers. But that's not what Jesus said in Matthew 24. To understand what Paul is saying here, we must go there.

Matthew 24:40-41 – *"Two men will be in the field; one will be taken* (παραλαμβάνεται–paralambanetai–taken away, removed, seized) *and the other left* (ἀφίεται–aphietai–left standing, tolerated, permitted). *Two women will be grinding with a hand mill; one will be taken* (παραλαμβάνεταὶ) *and the other left* (ᾱφίεται)."

The difficulty with the Rapture theology interpretation of these two verses is the context. Jesus says that his coming will be *"As it was in the days of Noah..."*, verse 37. He then goes on to explain what he means: *"For in the days before the flood, people were eating and drinking, marrying and giving in marriage, up to the day Noah entered the ark; and they knew nothing about what would happen until the flood came and <u>took them all away</u>* (ἦρεν–heren–took, removed, destroyed)."

Who was taken away? It was "them", those who *"knew nothing about what would happen"*. The flood "took them away", that is, washed them away and destroyed them. Keeping the meaning consistent, the man taken from the field and the woman taken from her hand mill were "swept away" or destroyed. Those who were left (left behind) were spared. Even though two different Greek words are used, to suggest that in the one place "taken away" means destroyed and a sentence later it means saved (or "raptured") is to be dishonest and inconsistent with the Scripture. Jesus does not say that Christians will be taken away, but that they will remain; they will be spared. It is plain from the context that Matthew 24:36-41is not a rapture text, but a judgement text. Thus "those who are alive and are left" in 1 Thessalonians 4:17 are the same as those who are "left behind" in Matthew 24:40-41.

The second issue with 1 Thessalonians 4:17 has to do with "meeting the Lord in the air". My question to my friend was "and then what?" And then *we shall be with the Lord forever*. Okay, we shall be with the Lord where? Paul does not say, and we cannot assume that we know from the immediate context. That means that we need to clarify from other places.

Let's begin with where we go when we die, since the first thing that happens in 1 Thessalonians 4:17 is that the dead are raised. There are several possible texts. Paul expresses a bit of confusion in Philippians 1:23 – *"I am torn between the two: I desire to depart and be with Christ, which is better by far, but it is more necessary for you that I remain in the body."*

Paul was convinced that if he died he would be with Christ. It still does not answer the question, for Paul does not say where Christ is. Hebrews 10:12 answers for us, *"But when this priest (Christ) had offered for all time one sacrifice for sins, he sat down at the right hand of God."*

John continues to clarify for us in Revelation 5:6, *"Then I saw a Lamb, looking as if it has been slain, standing in the center of the throne..."* This, of course is John's vision of heaven, as stated in Revelation 4:1. If we go to be with Jesus when we die, then it would seem clear that we go to heaven. Where is that? It is, to quote N. T. Wright, "God's space".[37]

I want to include in this part of the discussion a couple verses from Revelation 7. The first is the often mis-interpreted 144,000 of Revelation 7:4-8. We need to understand that the most important indication of meaning is the actual words on the page. John states quite clearly that the 144,000 were from the tribes of Israel. To emphasize that fact, he then enumerates the twelve tribes–though not precisely. Dan and Ephraim are omitted; Joseph and Levi are added. Joseph was the father of two tribes: Ephraim and Manasseh, making a total of thirteen tribes. However, Levi, being the priestly tribe, was not apportioned any territory in the Promised Land except priestly, or "Levitical", cities of refuge, and so the "territorial" tribes numbered twelve (see Joshua 13-21). Twelve tribes of Israel are listed in Revelation 7:5-8, with a "sealed" remnant of 12,000 from each tribe. It is plain that

---

[37] N. T. Wright, *Surprised by Hope* (New York: HarperCollins, 2008), pp111-116

John meant that the 144,000 were of the tribes of Israel and NOT of the Church. John apparently means to convey that God is keeping His promises to Israel and including them among the "saved".

> [*Just an aside:* We must accept that some righteous people were "saved" prior to the time of Christ. While we believe that there is (now) no salvation apart from faith in Christ, those who were righteous prior to Christ, such as Noah, Elijah, Elisha, Isaiah, etc., are apparently also saved. Both Paul, the writer of Hebrews and James use the righteousness of Abraham as an example of saving faith (Romans 4. Hebrews 11:8-19, James 2:23-24). If we understand that some righteous are saved, because of faith in God though not knowing of Christ, it is not difficult for us to accept Revelation 7:4-8 at face value. These are saved Jews, those of the tribes of Israel who are saved.

> There is, by the way, a second set of 144,000 who appear in Revelation 14:1-5. These had been *"purchased* (redeemed) *from the earth"*. They appear to be males who had been chaste (pure) and had not been with women. Their precise identification must remain a mystery to us for the time being. They sing a "new song"

that no one else is able to learn. Because of the severe limitation in numbers, it is plain that this cannot be all who are to be saved (though it is possible that this number represents a greater "whole". Analogical interpretations must be limited by the text and by the context: John does not specifically state that this is a representation, as he indicates metaphors in other places, Revelation 1:20 for example).]

Second is the great multitude of Revelation 7:9 – *"After this I looked and there before me was a great multitude that no one could count, from every nation, tribe, people and language, standing before the throne and in front of the Lamb. They were wearing white robes and were holding palm branches in their hands."* This great multitude is identified a few verses later (7:14) as those who *"have come out of the great tribulation"*, or affliction. Since the events that are commonly described as "The Great Tribulation" do not occur until several chapters later (11-16), I would suggest that John is talking about some other "great tribulation". Nor is this great multitude those who have been martyred for their faith. That group of worthies is depicted in Revelation 6:9 as waiting *"under the altar"* for their number to be completed. John has some other definition of "great affliction" for the 7:9 multitude.

I would suggest that since the Scriptures offer death as the punishment for sin, and *"in Adam all die"* (I Corinthians 15:22), and death is the last enemy to be destroyed (1 Corinthians 15:26), that John is talking about those who have "fallen asleep in Christ": the righteous who have died. We all fight death. Psychologists talk about the survival instinct. We spend billions of dollars to prolong life and delay death. Death is the one thing that virtually everyone fears. To walk through the valley of the shadow of death (Psalm 23:4) then, is the most fearsome affliction we face. In fact, it will be common to all men, regardless of their state of faith or their witness. John's *"great multitude that no one could count"* seems to be those who have died.

They are not sitting idly on clouds, wearing haloes and wings, and strumming golden harps. They are gathered around the great throne, singing praises to the one *"who sits on the throne, and to the Lamb"* (Revelation 7:10). These are the ones Paul says will be raised first, their souls united with recreated bodies. *"The dead in Christ will rise first. After that..."*

Having passed through death, gone to heaven to worship, and being raised to life, the dead in Christ will be joined by *"we who are alive and are left"*. Christ returns and we *"will be caught up together to meet the Lord in the air."* I return to my question – and then what?

Referring to the word *parousia* as describing Caesar's "coming", N. T. Wright goes on,

> And what happened at such a parousia was that the leading citizens would go out to meet him, the technical term for such a meeting being *apantçsis*, the word Paul uses

here for "meeting," as in "meeting the Lord in the air." But when the citizens went out to meet Caesar, they didn't stay there in the countryside. They didn't have a picnic in the fields and then bid him farewell; they went out *to escort their Lord royally into their city.*[38]

When someone comes to visit, what do we do? They knock at the door and announce their presence (1 Thessalonians 4:16–a loud command and a trumpet call). We respond by going to the door and opening it for them. Sometimes we see them coming. Relatives arrive in our driveway and we go out to meet them. But they did not come just to leave, and so our next action is...

We invite them into our homes. We bring them in and make them welcome. What happens after we meet the Lord in the air is that *"we will be with the Lord forever."* But the question was "Where will we be with the Lord?". For that we need to turn to Romans 8:18-23.

Here the same writer is making a point about the present in relation to the future: present sufferings in light of future glory. Notice the sense of frustration – The *creation waits in eager expectation...* (v 19). The *creation was subjected to frustration...* (v 20). The *hope that the creation itself will be liberated from its bondage to decay...* (v 21). *The whole creation has been groaning as in the pains of childbirth...* (v 22). Something is clearly wrong with the whole of

---

[38] Wright, *Surprised by Scripture*, p 101, emphasis his.

creation. Sin not only defaced the image of God in man but inflicted serious damage to the whole of God's creation. But the groaning comes with a note of hope.

In verse 19, creation is awaiting the revealing of the *"sons of God"*. In verse 21, it is awaiting liberation and *"the glorious freedom of the children of God."* And the very reason we endure the pains of childbirth is in the hope of the birth of a child (v 22). Paul goes on to say that *"we wait eagerly for our adoption as sons, the redemption of our bodies"* (v 23). He was looking forward to the day when God would finally redeem creation and set things to rights. What is Paul waiting for? What is creation anticipating?

They, and we, are waiting for what John describes in Revelation 21:1-3 as the new heaven and the new earth, and the passing away of the old. This is a re-creation. Peter wrote that *"The heavens will disappear with a roar; the elements will be destroyed by fire, and the earth and everything in it will be laid bare"* (2 Peter 3:10). The old will pass away and God will re-create new heavens and a new earth. But then (and this is the answer we've been waiting for), *"I saw the Holy City, the new Jerusalem, **coming down** out of heaven from God... And I heard a loud voice from the throne saying, 'Now **the dwelling of God is with men**, and he will live with them'"* (Revelation 21:3). The ultimate goal is not us going to heaven to be with God, but rather that God will recreate the heavens and the earth, and come down to dwell with us. The ultimate goal is not us abandoning earth and living for eternity in heaven, but rather God restoring His good creation, resurrecting the saints, and bringing the glory of heaven to earth. He comes down to us rather than taking us up to Him.

"And so," Paul says, *"We will be with the Lord forever"* (1 Thessalonians 4:17). Where? Not in heaven, but on a recreated earth. There is no "Rapture" that removes us from the earth; there is rather "Restoration" in which Christ returns to resurrected Christians living on a re-created earth.

How will this all happen? Well, two things. First, and perhaps most importantly, is the vital fact that *"every eye shall see him"*. Scripture clearly dispels of the myth of a *secret* rapture. The several places where the end (or the coming of Christ) occurs "as a thief" (Matthew 24:42-44; Luke 12:39; 1 Thessalonians 4:2-4; 2 Peter 3:10; Revelation 16:15) refer not to the secrecy of the Coming, but to its suddenness, and to its occurrence at an unexpected moment. That the return of Christ will be anything but a secret is evident in Jesus' own words and in John's reporting of his heavenly vision: ***"They will see** the Son of Man coming on the clouds..."* (Matthew 24:30). *"This same Jesus, who has been taken from you into heaven, will come back in **the same way you have seen him go** into heaven"* (Acts 1:11). *"Look, he is coming with the clouds, and **every eye will see him,** even those who pierced him..."* (Revelation 1:7).

Paul indicates that the destruction of the old and recreation of the new will be instantaneous: *"we will all be changed – in a flash, in the twinkling of an eye"* (1 Corinthians 15:51-52). In that moment the old heaven and old earth are destroyed and the new heaven and new earth are created. Genesis 1 tells us that God created with His spoken word. So the moment of creation is replicated with a moment of re-creation. In that moment, *"the dead will be raised imperishable, and we will all be changed"* (1 Corinthians 15:52), presumably, *"we who are alive and are left"*. Paul tells us that *"the perishable must clothe itself with the imperishable, and the mortal with immortality"* (1 Corinthians 15:53-54). That does not mean that we become insubstantial "spirit" beings, but that the substance of our creation is transformed (metamorphosed) from mortal and perishable to immortal and imperishable. In 1 Corinthians 15:35-49, Paul does not indicate that we cease to be "physical", but that we cease to be "natural". We are given recreated, restored bodies, of which the resurrection body of Christ is the first-fruit (1 Corinthians 15:20). The resurrection of Christ, then, is for Paul both a salvation event and a divine pledge for our own future. Because of Jesus' resurrection from the dead, we have life here and now, and we have the promise of resurrection and eternal life. Jesus' resurrection is the warranty of our hope.

To summarize, the Scripture is clear that there is no *secret* rapture, but also that there is no "Rapture", in which Christians are removed from the earth, at all. Rather, when we die, we cross to the other side of the room, to the other side of the veil, we "go to heaven" to be with Jesus and await the day of final judgment and resurrection which is promised to us in the resurrection of Jesus himself. When that final day comes, Jesus will return in an instant, visible to all, the dead will be raised, the living will join them. We will meet the Lord in the air as he returns. The old creation will be destroyed (2 Peter 3:10 uses a mixed image of destruction and the earth being "laid bare") so that new heavens and new earth will be created. We will all be given physical "resurrection" bodies that are immortal and imperishable. Then the new Jerusalem will descend to the new earth and God will come to be with us in that new creation. Our hope is not in escape but in the final restoration and reconciliation.

Paul concludes his letter with instruction that we should *"encourage each other with these words"* (1 Thessalonians 4:18) and *"encourage one another and build each other up"* (1 Thessalonians 5:11); with instructions to be watchful (1 Thessalonians 5:1-10) and to live holy and blameless lives (1Thessalonians 5:12-24). We are to live as resurrection people and in anticipation of the resurrection. We are to live as people of hope and promise and not as people of fear whose hope is in escape. We are to live as citizens of a kingdom that has come to us in promise and will one day come in all its resurrection glory. Our lives here and now are to be a foretaste for the world of what God has in store, that we bear witness to the kingdom of heaven in which *"the glory of God is its light, and the Lamb is its lamp"* (Revelation 21:23).

One final precautionary note: There are several End Times calendars that purport to show the sequence of final events. They will place the "Rapture" at various places depending on their interpretation of the Scriptures. And there are several names for the various ways of interpreting the Parousia (the unveiling) or the Apocalypse (the end). They will place events and people, such as the Beast, the Two Witnesses, the Millennial Reign, etc. along a time line. And they will all be adamant that their view is the correct one. As I have studied and tried to make sense of them, I find that they use verses from Daniel, Ezekiel, Isaiah, Zechariah, Matthew, 1 Thessalonians, 1 Peter, and Revelation, in many cases lifting phrases out of context, and then arranging and rearranging until they arrive at their chosen destination. I refer to this as "blender theology" because it seems that they have taken various apocalyptic writings, put them into a blender, and poured them out on a page. I find that, in general, the calendars make little sense when placed alongside the various scriptures *in context*. Some of them work very hard to arrive at a date for Christ's return. If one of them does happen to actually hit on the correct date of Christ's return, it will undoubtably be sheer chance. It is possible, after all, to hit all the numbers in a lottery. Somebody might win, slim as the odds may be. The fact remains that it is all guesswork. Only one knows the time of Christ's return (Matthew 24:36) – only the Father knows.

In recent days, there have been earthquakes–a magnitude 9.0 earthquake off the coast of Japan that caused a massive tsunami; a magnitude 6.5 earthquake near Vanuatu in the South Pacific. Whether these are "signs of the times" can only be a guess. There are wars and talks of war – for us, Iraq, Afghanistan, Syria – and international tensions. There have been volcanoes, hurricanes, famines and disasters of all sorts. Again, whether these are "signs of the times" is just a guess. Mankind has always been at war; the weather has always been unpredictable and violent; the earth has always, since the Great Flood, been "groaning as in the pains of childbirth".

Christians are not to live in fear, but to live in hope and as people of hope. And we are to live righteous lives in an unrighteous world, bringing light into the darkness. And we are to live in hope of the resurrection and restoration, not in anticipation of some grand escape. The Bible does not, in fact, teach that we shall escape through some "Rapture", but rather that we will be salt and light in this world until Christ returns with resurrection, reconciliation, and re-creation in his hands. We are people of hope who hold out the glorious hope of eternal resurrection to a lost, hopeless, and dying world. Let the Light shine. Sing out the songs of hope. Live the Kingdom Life.

14

Do All Dogs Go to Heaven?

Genesis 1-2; 9-10; Isaiah 11, 65; Revelation 21-22

I've been a pet owner most of my life. My parents tell me about a big, gentle furball of a cat that I would drag around by the tail when I was just a toddler. It's been mostly cats, like Sir Hillary, so named because he like to climb Mom's curtains. There've been mice–a white one named Blackie comes to mind. There was a parakeet that got away; some snakes and lizards, including one that got stepped on when I took it to school for "Show & Tell". There have also been fish and a dog or three along the way.

Tippy was a little wire-hair terrier who'd been mistreated. Marsha loved her and gentled her. When we married, Tippy welcomed me into her life, but, when our first child began to crawl it was more than the dog could tolerate. Tippy began to nip and growl. For the protection of our child, we made the painful decision to put Tippy to sleep.

We held her as she sighed her last sigh and slipped away to doggie heaven. I still regret that decision.

There was Rosie, an unclipped white Doberman Pinscher. Rosie was a big, gentle pound puppy who didn't look at all what she was. Her ears still flopped and her tail could sweep the coffee table clean. Sadly, we had to return her to the pound when a child in our church teased her to the point that she tried to attack him.

And there were others.

Along with pet ownership comes the inevitable parting. A beloved pet gets sick, or old, or injured, and dies. And we grieve. Even when their age or pain requires the mercy of euthanasia, we take that measure reluctantly and sorrowfully. And when a child experiences the death of a pet, the questions arise, "Do pets go to heaven?"

"Is my doggy with Jesus?"

"Daddy, where does my goldfish go when it dies?"

And, believe me, "in the toilet" is not an acceptable answer. The proper answer is to give the pet a proper burial, complete with a shoebox "casket" and a properly solemn funeral service with all the trappings. It also helps if you answer as this gentleman did:

"Would you be happy in heaven if your puppy wasn't there?"

"No." the child answered.

"Well," the man replied, "You will be happy in heaven."

The death of a pet raises perhaps the most profound theological conundrum for a child – and for any sensitive parent trying to comfort a grieving child: Do animals have souls? Where do pets go when they die?

The Bible has an answer.

To the first question (do animals have souls?), it is tempting to answer, No. Genesis 1 and 2 are creation accounts, and, for our purposes, Genesis 1 relates the creation of animals. Verse 20 begins, *And God said, "Let the waters team with living creatures, and let birds fly above the earth and in the expanse of the sky." So God created...* Then verse 24, And God said, *"Let the land produce living creatures according to their kinds..."* It appears that God merely spoke them into existence, just as he did the stars, trees, and the light. Genesis 1:26-27 appears to relate the creation of humanity in the same way. However, Genesis 2:7 has a more elaborate and interesting description of the creation of humanity, not duplicated in relation to animals: *the LORD God formed the man from the dust of the ground and breathed into his nostrils the breath* (spirit) *of life, and the man became a living being* (soul).

We take that to indicate the uniqueness of humanity as distinct from the animal kingdom. But this idea cannot be based on this verse. In chapter one, the same Hebrew phrase, "living being" (which may also be translated "living soul"), is translated "living creatures". Using the same phrase, and translating consistently, would lead one to the conclusion that "living creatures" and "living beings" are the same. That is, that man (in the generic sense) as a "living being" is not different from the animals as "living creatures". Both are "living souls" or "living beings".

The Teacher, writing in Ecclesiastes, suggests that there is really no difference between man and animal. Man is like the animals and has the same fate. *All have the same breath... All go to the same place* (the grave is implied). Then the Teacher asks, *"Who knows if the spirit of man rises upward and if the spirit of the animal goes down into the earth?"* (Ecclesiastes 3:18-21). The general tone of Ecclesiastes is dark and dismal, but the author used that same word, breath, that is also translated *spirit* or *wind*, that was used in Genesis.

The uniqueness of humanity is encapsulated in the *imago dei* (the Image of God), that phrase in 1:26-27 depicting mankind as being created in the *image* and *likeness* of the Creator. It is that distinction, rather than the presence, or existence, of a "soul", that makes mankind unique. God created mankind to be in his image, with more than just physical existence. God took care to create a like image, with qualities that set him apart from the rest of creation: a moral nature, a rational nature, free will, intellect, and in communion (fellowship) with his Creator. In addition to the "likeness", there is the added dimension of the "breath (or *spirit*) of life", that God endowed mankind with his divine breath. Lest that be too confusing, it should be noted that in both Hebrew and Greek, the same words may be translated *breath, wind,* or *spirit*. So, where God spoke creatures into being, he breathed life into mankind. We might say, then, that mankind has a *spirit*, whereas the creatures do not.

In contrast to the rest of creation, including the birds, fish, and other "creeping things", mankind appears to *be* (not to *have*) a soul. The simple answer, usually, is that animals do not have souls, in the religious sense of a "spiritual nature". And when I have broached the subject with other Christians, they almost immediately jump to this conclusion.

However, the Genesis account, because of its poetic structure, is incomplete. It does not tell us everything we wish to know about creation. To be perfectly honest, then, we simply don't know whether or not animals have souls. The creation account doesn't tell us one way or the other, and the text does not unambiguously support the traditional interpretation. Making dogmatic statements based on the absence of evidence is unwise.

We do know that animals seem to have emotions: they respond to affection and show it; they feel fear; and they respond when they are irritated. There appears to be more there than just instinct and stimulus/response. Some scientists like to talk and write about the similarities between humanity and animals of various species. The similarities are interesting, but the differences are profound. In terms of creativity, intellect, and morality, mankind is unique in the "animal" kingdom. But, to the question of whether animals have souls, in the same way we think humans have, we truly don't know.

There is something we do know. In the Genesis 1 account, God responds to the creation of the animals, both to creatures of the sea and air and to creatures of the land with this: *And God saw that it was good* (vv 21 & 25). In a final summary statement, the writer of Genesis records, *God saw all that he had made, and it was very good* (v. 31).

An interesting dimension comes to the fore in the account of the great flood (Genesis 6-9). In the face of the profound sinfulness of mankind, God took special care to preserve representative animals. Following the Genesis 3 account of the rebellion of mankind, Genesis 6:5 recounts that *the LORD saw how great man's wickedness on the earth had become, and that every inclination of the thoughts of his heart was only evil all the time.* God proposes to preserve his creation, the best of it, by destroying the worst of it. The flood was to wipe away all humanity except Noah, who *found favor in the eyes of the LORD* (Genesis 6:8).

If repetition indicates a level of importance or value, then the number of times that the animals are mentioned in the flood account may give us some idea of the measure of God's concern for the "very good" animals he had created. Take a look:

Twice, God included animals in the plan of destruction: Genesis 6:7 and 17, and twice, in Genesis 7:23-24, the death of the animals outside the ark is noted. But God's plan of salvation included the animals. Just as he would preserve Noah's family, so he would preserve representative animals.

> Genesis 6:19-20 – *You are to bring into the ark two of all living creatures, male and female, to keep them alive with you. Two of every kind of bird, of every kind of animal and of every kind of creature that moves along the ground will come to you to be kept alive.*

Genesis 7:2-3 – *Take with you seven[39] of every kind of clean animal a male and its mate, and two of every kind of unclean animal, a male and its mate, and also seven of every kind of bird, male and female, to keep their various kinds alive throughout the earth.*

Genesis 7:8-9 – *Pairs of clean and unclean animals, of birds and of all creatures that move along the ground, male and female, came to Noah and entered the ark, as God had commanded Noah.*

Genesis 7:14-16 – *They had with them (on the ark) every wild animal according to its kind, all livestock according to their kinds, every creature that moves along the ground according to its kind and every bird according to its kind, everything with wings. Pairs of all creatures that have the breath of life in them came to Noah and entered the ark. The animals going in were male and female of every living thing, as God had commanded Noah.*

After the flood, Genesis 8:1 – *But God remembered Noah and all the wild animals and the livestock that were with him in the ark...* And then, in verse 17, Noah is to bring the animals out of the ark with him. It would appear that the animals are very

---

[39] Or, *seven pairs*

important to God. Even though he didn't save them all, God took special care to save some of each kind.

Our vision of heaven is largely based on Revelation 21 and 22, the final reconciliation of all creation into a "new heaven and a new earth" with God present. But there is an earlier "preview" of heaven found in Isaiah 65. Verse 17 begins, *"Behold, I will create new heavens and a new earth."* From verse 13, we are to understand that these are the words of God. We naturally tend to read this from a human view, with such promises as no more infant mortality, and extremely long age: *"Never again will there be in it an infant who lives but a few days, or an old man who does not live out his years; he who dies at a hundred will be thought a mere youth..."*

While this is a beatific vision for humanity, we note that it also includes animals. The problem with this is that we interpret the animals almost metaphorically as mere symbols of a peaceful existence for us. The writer of Isaiah 65 did not view it that way, though. This paradisaical age includes this: *"The wolf and the lamb will feed together, and the lion will eat straw like the ox... they will neither harm nor destroy on all my holy mountain," says the LORD* (Isaiah 65:25).

Prior to that, Isaiah has a vision regarding a person he refers to as "a branch", *a shoot [that] will spring from the stem of Jesse* (Isaiah 11:1). This is a Messianic prophecy that we understand as referring to Jesus. But this appears to also be a prophecy regarding an idyllic age of peace, perhaps, along with Isaiah 65 the sort of paradise we find in Revelation 21-22. Here, Isaiah also refers to animals occupying a place in "heaven" –

> *And the wolf will dwell with the lamb, and the leopard will lie down with the kid, and the calf and the young lion and the fatling together; and a little boy will lead them. Also the cow and the bear will graze; their young will lie down together; and the lion will eat straw like the ox. And the nursing child will play by the hold of the cobra, and the weaned child will put his hand on the viper's den. They will not hurt or destroy in all My holy mountain, for the earth will be full of the knowledge of the LORD as the waters cover the sea* (Isaiah 11:6-9, NASB).

There appear to be many parallels between Isaiah 11 and 65 and Revelation 21-22, and while animals are not mentioned in the Revelation, the indications from Isaiah are that animals are certain to be present in the restored creation. Their appearance in the prophecy should not be construed as merely metaphorical, but that their behaviors are in keeping with the New Creation. And that leads me to this conclusion: animals are very much a part of God's good creation; they are under God's care; they are part of God's eternal plan; and, they will be present in God's restored creation. The issue for us is not really whether animals have souls – or spirits – but the reality presented in the Bible that God includes them, not only in the beginning and the present world, but in the "new heaven and new earth" as well.

I don't think it is false to reassure your child: Yes, your puppy, your kitty is in heaven. Yes, your goldfish and gerbil, too. Along with wolves (which are just wild dogs), leopards and lions (which are just wild cats), sheep, goats...

And children.

Index of Scripture References

Exodus 19:4-6
Numbers 2
Deuteronomy18:15, 18
Nehemiah 8:10
Isaiah 7:14; 29:13
Daniel 11
Hosea 11:1
Micah 3:14; 5:2
Malachi 2:2
Matthew 1:21; 2:2-3
John 1:1-18; 4:24
Philippians 2:6-11

Chapter 6
Genesis 12:3
Exodus 16:4; 17:1-7; 19:4-6
Psalm 36:8; 46:4
Isaiah 66:12
Matthew 3; 3:15; 5:14-16; 28:18-20
Mark 1
Luke 3
John 2, 3, 4, 5, 6, 7
John 1:12, 33; 3:3, 5; 4:4-15; 7:37-38; 9:1-11
Romans 6:16-18
1 Corinthians 10:4
2 Corinthians 3:18; 5:21
1 Peter 2:9-10

Chapter 7
Genesis 8:4-11
Exodus 3:1ff; 13:21; 17:1-7; 19:6; 24:17

Leviticus 6:8-13; 11:44-45; 19:1; 20:7
Deuteronomy 4:24
Judges 6:20-22
2 Samuel 22:9
1 Kings 18:16-42
1 Chronicles 21:26
2 Chronicles 7:1
Psalms 18; 24:3-4; 51:10
Isaiah 6:7; 30:26-28; 33:14
Jeremiah 9:7
Daniel 3
Jonah 1:17
Zechariah 13:9
Malachi 3:3
Matthew 3:11; 5:12, 48; 12:38-40
Mark 15:44-45
Luke 24:41-43
John 1:14, 17; 3:22; 7:37
Acts 1:3; 2:1-18
Romans 6:4; 8:2
1 Corinthians 1:2; 10:4; 15:3-8
2 Corinthians 5:17
1 Thessalonians 4:3
Hebrews 12:1, 10, 14, 18, 22, 24, 28-29; 13:12
1 Peter 1:15-16; 2:4-9

Chapter 8
Genesis 1:31; 2:10; 3:14-19, 22
Exodus 19:6

1 Samuel 10:10
2 Chronicles 15:1;
20:14; 24:20
Jeremiah31:34
Matthew 4:1-11; 14:22
Mark 1:12-13
Luke 1:15, 41, 67;
3:22; 4:1-13
John 1:14; 14:26; 15:26;
16:8,13-14
Acts 1:8
Romans 10:9
1 Corinthians 10:13
2 Corinthians 5:21
Hebrews 5:8-9; 8:12;
10:17; 12:6
1 John 1:9; 2:1

Chapter 12
Exodus 15; 16:1-36
Deuteronomy 8:3-5; 15-18
Proverbs 3:11-12
Matthew4:1-11; 6:11, 25;
7:11; 14:13-20; 15:29-39;
John 1:1-4; 6:35, 63b
1 Corinthians 10:13
Hebrews 4:15; 5:8; 12:5
James 1:2-4

Chapter 13
Psalm 23:4
Daniel 11
Matthew 24:30, 36-41,42-44
Luke12:39
John 16:33
Acts 1:11
Romans 4; 8:18-23
1 Corinthians 15:22, 26,
35-59,51-52, 53-54
Philippians 1:23
1 Thessalonians 4:2-4,16, 17;
5:1-10, 11, 12-24
Hebrews 10:12; 11:8-19
James 2:23-24
2 Peter 3:10
Revelation 1:7; 4:1; 7:4-8,
9, 10, 14; 14:1-5; 16:15;
21:1-3, 23

Chapter 14
Genesis 1;20, 21, 25,
26-27, 31; 2:7; 3; 6:5, 7, 8,
19-20; 7:2-3, 8-9, 14-16,
23-24; 8:1 9-10
Ecclesiastes 3:18-21
Isaiah 11;1,6-9, 65;13, 17, 25
Revelation 21-22

BIBLIOGRAPHY

Cahill, Thomas, *The Gifts of the Jews* (New York: Anchor Books, 1998)

Edidin, Ben M., *Jewish Customs and Ceremonies* (New York: Hebrew Publishing Company, 1941)

Edwards, James R., *Is Jesus the Only Savior?* (Grand Rapids: William B. Eerdmans Company, 2005)

Honeycutt, Frank G., *Marry a Pregnant Virgin* (Minneapolis: Augsburg Fortress, 2008)

Lewis, C. S., *The Great Divorce* (New York: HarperCollins, 2000)

Mayfield, Joseph H., "John", *Beacon Bible Commentary, Volume 7* (Kansas City: Beacon Hill Press of Kansas City, 1965)

McMahon, Regan, "Everybody Does It", September 6, 2007, http://www.sfgate.com/education/article/Everybody-Does-It-2523376.php OR, http://www.wahooschools.org/vnews/display.v/ART/2007/10/03/4703b9e9ebf36

Roettgers, Janko, "Piracy: Everybody Does It; Everything Should Be Free", Feb. 16,

2011, http://gigaom.com/2011/02/16/
piracy-consumer-attitudes/

Sendak, Maurice, *Where the Wild Things Are* (New
York: HarperCollins, 1963)

Walton, John H., *The Lost World of Genesis One*
(Downers Grove: InterVarsity Press, 2009)

Wright, N. T., *Surprised by Hope: Rethinking Heaven,
the Resurrection, and the Mission of the Church*
(New York: HarperCollins, 2008)

Wright, N. T., *Surprised by Scripture:
Engaging Contemporary Issues* (New York,
HarperCollins, 2014)